SpringerBriefs in Political Science

SpringerBriefs present concise summaries of cutting-edge research and practical applications across a wide spectrum of fields. Featuring compact volumes of 50 to 125 pages, the series covers a range of content from professional to academic. Typical topics might include:

- A timely report of state-of-the art analytical techniques
- A bridge between new research results, as published in journal articles, and a contextual literature review
- A snapshot of a hot or emerging topic
- An in-depth case study or clinical example
- A presentation of core concepts that students must understand in order to make independent contributions

SpringerBriefs in Political Science showcase emerging theory, empirical research, and practical application in political science, policy studies, political economy, public administration, political philosophy, international relations, and related fields, from a global author community.

SpringerBriefs are characterized by fast, global electronic dissemination, standard publishing contracts, standardized manuscript preparation and formatting guidelines, and expedited production schedules.

Anja Mihr · Cindy Wittke
Editors

Human Rights Dissemination in Central Asia

Human Rights Education and Capacity Building in the Post-Soviet Space

Editors
Anja Mihr
OSCE Academy in Bishkek
Bishkek, Kyrgyzstan

Cindy Wittke
Leibniz Institute for East and Southeast
European Studies (IOS)
Regensburg, Germany

ISSN 2191-5466   ISSN 2191-5474 (electronic)
SpringerBriefs in Political Science
ISBN 978-3-031-27971-3   ISBN 978-3-031-27972-0 (eBook)
https://doi.org/10.1007/978-3-031-27972-0

© The Editor(s) (if applicable) and The Author(s) 2023. This book is an open access publication.
Open Access This book is licensed under the terms of the Creative Commons Attribution 4.0 International License (http://creativecommons.org/licenses/by/4.0/), which permits use, sharing, adaptation, distribution and reproduction in any medium or format, as long as you give appropriate credit to the original author(s) and the source, provide a link to the Creative Commons license and indicate if changes were made.

The images or other third party material in this book are included in the book's Creative Commons license, unless indicated otherwise in a credit line to the material. If material is not included in the book's Creative Commons license and your intended use is not permitted by statutory regulation or exceeds the permitted use, you will need to obtain permission directly from the copyright holder.

The use of general descriptive names, registered names, trademarks, service marks, etc. in this publication does not imply, even in the absence of a specific statement, that such names are exempt from the relevant protective laws and regulations and therefore free for general use.

The publisher, the authors, and the editors are safe to assume that the advice and information in this book are believed to be true and accurate at the date of publication. Neither the publisher nor the authors or the editors give a warranty, expressed or implied, with respect to the material contained herein or for any errors or omissions that may have been made. The publisher remains neutral with regard to jurisdictional claims in published maps and institutional affiliations.

This Springer imprint is published by the registered company Springer Nature Switzerland AG
The registered company address is: Gewerbestrasse 11, 6330 Cham, Switzerland

Preface

In December 2022, the United Nations celebrated the 10th anniversary of the UN Declaration for Human Rights Education and Learning at the Global Forum on Human Rights Education held in Samarkand, Uzbekistan. For the first time in UN history, such a forum was held in Central Asia, supported by the Uzbek government and various international organizations. The Forum highlighted the 'importance of human rights is an integral part of any training or educational program'.[1]

Over the past decade, remarkable efforts have been made by international organizations, civil society, and higher education institutions in the Central Asian countries of Kazakhstan, Kyrgyzstan, and Uzbekistan and to some extent in Tajikistan to make human rights a central part of education. Despite the undeniable difficulties that current political regimes, (frozen) conflicts and the legacies of Soviet authoritarian leadership are posing to promote and disseminate human rights in Central Asia, non-governmental organizations in alliance with local human rights defenders, civil society and international organizations have been at the forefront in promoting, financing, and disseminating materials, conducting trainings and supporting governmental actions plans for human rights and curricula development for universities.

This edited volume pays tribute to these developments. In nine chapters, the authors provide an overview and reflect on the efforts by different actors and organizations to disseminate international human rights standards through education and awareness-raising programs in accordance with the commitments that governments in the region have made to human rights when becoming a member of the United Nations and other international organizations such as the Organizations for Security and Cooperation in Europe (OSCE).

The compendium starts with general overviews of human rights education and compliance in Central Asia, it makes the tensions between internationalization and nation-building visible and discusses the challenges and perspectives for the future.

---

[1] Global Forum on Human Rights Education, 5–6 December 2022, Samarkand, Uzbekistan; https://www.unodc.org/centralasia/en/global-forum-on-human-rights-education-in-uzbekistan.html (accessed January 2023).

It also illustrates the shortcomings and domestic limits for human rights in legal education and adjudication in some countries but also highlights the modest progress made through empowerment and awareness overall for the human rights of women, children, and migrants.

This open access publication was realized thanks to the generous grant by the DAAD's East West Dialogue program for the project "Human Rights in Central Asia: Between Nation-Building and Internationalization" ("Menschenrechte in Zentralasien: Zwischen Nationsbildung &Internationalisierung", project-ID: 57570215) and the project "Between Conflict and Cooperation: The Politics of International Law in the Post-Soviet Space" (Zwischen Konflikt und Kooperation: Politiken des Völkerrechts im post-sowjetischen Raum" (PolVR), project-ID: 01UC1901) at the Leibniz Institute for East and Southeast European Studies (IOS) in Regensburg (https://leibniz-ios.de/en/) funded by the German Federal Ministry of Education and Research (BMBF). In addition, the OSCE Academy in Bishkek supported and co-founded the realization of the workshops in Bishkek and the research in Central Asia over the past years.

Bishkek, Kyrgyzstan Anja Mihr
Regensburg, Germany Cindy Wittke
January 2023

Contents

Foreword

Human Rights Dissemination in Central Asia—Between Internationalization and Nation-Building 3
Melanie Hien, Florian Kuebler, and Aikerim Nazaralieva

Human Rights in Central Asia - Challenges and Perspectives 15
Sergey Sayapin

Human Rights Education in Central Asia 31
Anja Mihr

Human Rights as a Concept of Public Law: Challenges for Central Asian Higher Education Systems 47
Rustam Atadjanov

Transnational Higher Education—The Case of Kazakhstan 61
Eriks Varpahovskis and Anna Kuteleva

Redesigning the Law Curriculum in Uzbekistan 73
Aziz Ismatov and Manuchehr Kudratov

Inclusive Human Rights Education in Tajikistan 89
Mohirakhoni Husnidinzoda

Awareness in Central Asian States of Discrimination Against Labor Migrants 105
Kasiet Ysmanova

Gender Equality and International Human Rights Law in Kyrgyzstan 115
Aizhan Erisheva

Annex 129

Foreword

Human Rights Dissemination in Central Asia—Between Internationalization and Nation-Building

Melanie Hien, Florian Kuebler, and Aikerim Nazaralieva

1 Introduction

Since the collapse of the Soviet Union, human rights education and knowledge dissemination in Central Asia has passed through different stages of development. The mix of democratic and authoritarian, as well as autocratic systems in the region poses challenges, in particular for human rights defenders (HRDs). Over the course of the last three decades, the opportunities open to these activists have changed, either becoming more limited or broader, depending on the governments and characteristics of the country's political system. In response to this, in 2021, the Leibniz Institute for East and Southeast European Studies (IOS) in Regensburg, Germany, and the OSCE Academy in Bishkek, Kyrgyzstan, jointly implemented a project on "Human Rights in Central Asia—Between Internationalization and Nation-Building," funded by the German Academic Exchange Service (DAAD). The objective[1] of this research project and its workshops, which took place in a hybrid format from 4 to 8 October 2021 in Bishkek, was to explore the dissemination of knowledge on human rights, human rights policies, and empowerment, as well as human rights education in the context of processes of transformation, state-building, and nation-building in the states of Central Asia since the 1990s. The one-week workshop, designed for both civil society activists and young professionals, included open lectures on human

---

[1] A second objective was to create a network of established academics and young scholars and professionals from Kazakhstan, Kyrgyzstan, Tajikistan, Uzbekistan, and Turkmenistan to develop—jointly with civil society organizations and academics—educational and training material (in print and electronic form) to contribute to human rights empowerment in all five Central Asian states.

M. Hien · F. Kuebler (✉) · A. Nazaralieva
University of Regensburg, Regensburg, Germany
e-mail: FlorianKueble96@gmx.de

M. Hien
e-mail: melanie.hien@gmx.de

© The Author(s) 2023
A. Mihr and C. Wittke (eds.), *Human Rights Dissemination in Central Asia*, SpringerBriefs in Political Science,
https://doi.org/10.1007/978-3-031-27972-0_1

rights, human rights education, data protection, and European Union (EU) programs on human rights in Central Asia, as well as keynote speeches, which were open to the public.

This article provides a review of the observations and lessons learned from the workshops conducted regarding human rights education and knowledge dissemination in Central Asia, including the vital or exclusory role played by the expertise of civil society activists in the countries of the region. In the first part of the article, we summarize the key discussion outcomes from the two workshops, including human rights instruments and legislation pertaining to Civil Society Organizations (CSOs).[2] In the following we outline the lessons learned in the sphere of human rights education and knowledge dissemination, with regard to materials and teaching, and both the role of academia and social media usage. This is followed by an overview of the role of civil societies in the region in the context of human rights education. In the next part of the article, we summarize the aspects of the sustainability of CSO projects and measurement of their impact. All this demonstrates not only a lack of knowledge on human rights-related issues in the region, but also the paucity of human rights education and material needed to enable effective knowledge dissemination and education on human rights in the Central Asian states. Drawing these points together, in the last chapter of the article, we formulate a set of recommendations for domestic, regional, and international state and non-state actors of human rights knowledge dissemination working in, with, and on the region, before concluding with our main findings.

2 Human Rights Instruments and ivil Society Legislation

2.1 *Human Rights Instruments*

The knowledge of *human rights instruments*,[3] signed and ratified by the countries in Central Asia, is limited and varies from country to country, partly depending on the characteristics of their political system. That said, no educational efforts have been made to provide this knowledge. Information and education are therefore needed to raise the awareness of people in the region about their rights and how to exercise them.

Not only are people less informed, but there is also a prevailing view in the region that human rights education and knowledge dissemination is a westernized, top-down

---

[2] Following Diamond (1994), it is important to note that there is a difference between "CSO" and "NGO," in that the latter does not encompass all organizations that belong to civil society. Accordingly, in this article, NGO refers to the term "non-governmental organization" meaning an independent organization with non-state funding, including foreign funding sources.

[3] For a detailed overview of human rights instruments and treaties in the respective countries of Central Asia, see: https://www.tbinternet.ohchr.org/_layouts/15/TreatyBodyExternal/Treaty.aspx?CountryID=180&Lang=EN.

approach. The resulting bias in society means that people are not informed about the international obligations their governments took on when signing treaties related to human rights issues. In contrast, government officials often work against these rights and civil society's commitment to protecting them, for example by labeling organizations foreign agents or interrupting the workshops held by activists. Consequently, raising awareness and training people to conduct human rights education and knowledge dissemination to counter governments' actions and accusations is essential.

2.2 Civil Society Organization-Related Legislation

Besides the human rights treaties, legislation targeting Civil Society Organizations (CSOs) and how they are treated varies across the region. Russia's influence on the Central Asian states and the extent to which the country could serve as a law-making role model for the region, particularly in the civil society sphere—with legislation such as the "foreign agent law"—is therefore a matter of discussion and concern. Although there are no such foreign agent laws in the countries of Central Asia, experts assume reporting requirements and schemes in the respective countries to be in the tradition of such a law and CSOs and activists are, in practice, being labeled or referred to as foreign agents. This is something that happens during workshops, for instance, which are often interrupted by officials, or in the media. In this section, we provide a short overview of the legislation in Central Asia that is related to CSOs and is assumed to be in the tradition of Russia's foreign agent law.

In *Kyrgyzstan*, for example, according to a report by the organization International Partnership for Human Rights, there is no law that treats CSOs as foreign agents (IPHR 2021a).[4] However, in 2021, amendments to the Law on Non-Commercial Organizations (NCOs) raised concerns in the international community about a new financial reporting scheme requiring CSOs to submit annual information regarding their funding to the Ministry of Justice. This additional workload will most certainly have an impact on the effectiveness of Kyrgyz CSOs (UN Special Rapporteur 2022). Government critics have also been intimidated and harassed in the past (IPHR 2021b). Similarly, in *Tajikistan*, the Law on Public Associations requires that these organizations provide detailed information on the types and sources of funding they receive,

---

[4] As the International Partnership for Human Rights points out: "It requires NGOs to prepare and submit annually a report about their sources of funding, how they spend these funds, as well as their acquisition and use of property for publication on the website of the state tax service. This will increase an already heavy reporting burden for NGOs, especially small organizations with limited staff and resources. The new requirements only apply to NGOs, not to other non-profit or commercial organizations, making them discriminatory in nature. The failure of NGOs to comply with the new reporting obligations may result in penalties, including the closure of organizations." International Partnership for Human Rights (2021). Kyrgyzstan update: Restrictive "false" info and NGO laws adopted, intimidation of government critics. https://www.iphronline.org/kyrgyzstan-upd ate-restrictive-false-info-and-ngo-laws-adopted-intimidation-of-government-critics.html .

as well as their beneficiaries and partners. All foreign funding must be registered with the Ministry of Justice. According to the Ministry, in 2020, more than 100 organizations were denied registration due to missing information (IPHR 2021c). Missing reports about foreign funding have also been used against CSOs in *Kazakhstan* in recent years to suspend their activities for a certain amount of time. There have been various cases of individual activists being charged with broad criminal offenses—such as involvement in extremist groups and inciting discord (IPHR 2021b). Civil society organizations in *Uzbekistan* also face difficulties with bureaucratic registration requirements, including many reasons for the government to deny official registration (IPHR 2021d). There have been recent crackdowns on protests, unregistered organizations, and individuals affiliated to them (Freedom House 2021). Even though, over the past few years, we witnessed a gradual process of opening up of the political system, including the adoption of a Concept on Development of Civil Society 2021 for 2021–2025, activists and CSOs still cannot carry out their work without facing repression (HRW 2020a). In *Turkmenistan*, too, CSOs operate under difficult circumstances. There is only very limited space for civil society and organizations cannot operate openly in the country (HRW 2020b). Activists have been imprisoned on various charges, such as hooliganism or fraud (Civicus 2022).

In other words, the situation remains challenging in all Central Asian countries. Although there are no foreign agent laws comparable to Russia's, the Central Asian regimes find plenty of ways to limit the space in which CSOs can operate and to silence activists.

3 Human Rights Education and Knowledge Dissemination

Human rights education and knowledge dissemination in Central Asia is not only dependent on knowledge of the human rights treaties or CSO-related legislation, but also on the resources organizations have at their disposal to educate people and raise awareness about human rights and how individuals can exercise those rights. These resources are summarized in the following sections.

3.1 Teaching and Material

When it comes to *teaching* human rights, there is a continuing need to educate human rights trainers. This is especially important as the countries in Central Asia are multilingual and there is a lack of trainers in country-specific languages. In this respect, there is also a gap between rural and urban areas. As there are fewer human rights teachers in rural areas, there is even less human rights education there. Another issue that must be remedied is the scarcity of data collected on human rights-related issues, such as violations. It is therefore important to support organizations by providing documentation of these violations, including, *inter alia*, statistics. Similarly, CSOs need help to improve their sustainability, for instance by developing their organizational and professional structures to address their lack of knowledge and experience. Hence, further training and specialization of organizations is essential to meet their needs and improve the quality of their operations.

At the same time, media education and media literacy should be part of human rights education and training in the region, as most communication between organizations and participants or volunteers, as well as within organizations, takes place online. In this context, it is important to raise awareness about how to handle sensitive data online. Regarding the collection of information from the media and literature on human rights, it is also important that human rights trainers and participants in their projects have a basic understanding of how the media works, and which media outlets can be trusted.

Concerning the *material* for human rights education, there is a lack of textbooks in different languages in Central Asia. Those that are available tend to be written in Russian but not in national languages. The use of outdated editions from the former Soviet Union causes problems, as human rights standards have changed dramatically in the region since the collapse of the USSR. Hence, there is a need to support the development and publication of human rights textbooks, both in Russian and the national languages, to enable broad human rights education. Another linguistic aspect in the field of human rights education is the need for material written in plain language, accessible and understandable for everyone, but at the same time not so over-simplified that it loses its meaning. It is also important for human rights education to not only be focused on children and young students, but adults should be able to benefit from it, too. Consequently, material must target adults as much as children. This could also improve existing education concepts and have a lasting impact on them, which, especially in rural regions in Central Asia, would make a useful contribution to reaching a broader audience (Transparency International 2021).

Beyond this, it is crucial to develop education material, such as human rights ranking and overviews, in the local and regional contexts in Central Asia. This also includes the abovementioned collection of data on human rights and human rights violations by government authorities. There is a shortage of such material in the region, and little is being done to develop it. Consequently, organizations and individual activists in the field of human rights and human rights education should be helped to adapt material from international bodies, such as the United Nations (UN), or even human rights material from the EU.

3.2 Academia

In *academia* in Central Asia there is a lack of knowledge about the human rights instruments that apply both within the respective states and in the neighboring countries. There is barely any information about the human rights treaties and the countries' obligations under them. It is therefore important to improve the knowledge and expertise within the region about human rights, human rights instruments, and their implementation. Standardized indicators measuring the extent to which human rights are observed or violated throughout the region could facilitate cooperation between academia and governments. Further, creating networks between scholars in the field of human rights is essential to improve research in the field. In the following, we will provide an overview of the situation in the branches of academia focused on human rights.

International law and human rights are rarely offered as majors in Central Asian universities.[5] To summarize the situation: In Kazakhstan, there are a total of 150 universities but only five of the leading institutions offer International Law as a subject. Only three of the 39 universities in Tajikistan have courses enabling students to focus on this major. The situation in Turkmenistan is similar, with three of 42 universities offering International Law as a bachelor's degree. Uzbekistan has 57 universities, of which four have departments of International Law. In Kyrgyzstan, there are 64 universities, of which five offer a focus on International Law. The only university in the country that provides a Liberal Arts Human Rights Concentration is the American University of Central Asia (AUCA). Other universities do not have departments devoted to human rights. Nevertheless, the state universities do hold roundtables to discuss human rights issues in the country on International Human Rights Day.

3.3 Social Media Usage

Human rights education and knowledge dissemination also includes the tools organizations use to spread information in the region. The sharing of information by activists in Central Asia is mostly done online, i.e., on social media platforms. The lack of transparency of certain media companies therefore makes this difficult. Cybersecurity is an area where people in Central Asia are not familiar with their rights or how to exercise these. Nor are they aware of their digital footprint or vulnerability when sending sensitive information via the internet. Internet companies use artificial intelligence to filter and promote information sources, whereby misleading information and the misuse of data is a frequent occurrence. Moreover, the regulations of these companies are difficult to access or understand and can therefore not really be opposed. As these platforms are sometimes the only way to connect with people,

---

[5] This information was collected from the following university websites: Kazahkstan: https://www.kls.kazguu.kz/en/, https://www.kimep.kz/school-of-law/en/, https://www.yur.enu.kz, https://www.kaznu.kz/en/357/page/%20Departments/Law_Faculty, http://www.kriu.edu.kz/en/department/department-of-training-law/; Tajikistan: http://www.rtsu.tj, https://www.tnu.tj/wp-content/uploads/2020/09/faculty-of-law.pdf, http://www.tsulbp.tj/glavnaya; Turkmenistan: https://www.mfa.gov.tm/en/articles/51?breadcrumbs=no, https://www.tdu.edu.tm/?/Faculty%20of%20Law/&page=19&in=69, https://www.iuhd.edu.tm/faculty/4; Uzbekistan: https://www.uwed.uz/en/faculties/international-law, https://www.tsul.uz/uz/general-page/Faculty%20of%20Law-QS, https://www.samdu.uz.

especially in rural or remote areas, these conditions jeopardize the safety of human rights activists.

Beyond this, CSOs in Central Asia are often under surveillance and are subject to controls carried out by government officials, frequently during digital workshop sessions. The organizations are unable to prevent these interruptions, which once again increases their vulnerability.

4 The Vital Role of Expertise in Central Asian Civil Societies

In line with the discussions about human rights education and knowledge dissemination in Central Asia, we also see the importance of *the vital (or exclusory) role that expertise plays in the civil societies of the countries* of Central Asia. Civil society organizations are more active than the states themselves when it comes to providing education and disseminating knowledge on human rights in Central Asia and are therefore helping to change prevailing traditions. Despite government officials interrupting workshops or the negative public debate about foreign-funded organizations, activists engage in various fields throughout the region, including the empowerment of women or the education of children. For these areas of work, CSOs develop their own tools, e.g., educational games to teach about human rights.

An important example illustrating the necessity of civil society is women's engagement in local development. Women are underrepresented in this field, especially in municipal councils. To increase the number of women involved, cooperation with municipalities, legislation, and the empowerment of women are important parameters. It is therefore crucial to integrate the gender dimension in the activities and legislation of local self-government bodies and thus to raise awareness of gender issues, a goal that organizations are actively pursuing throughout the region. Furthermore, legislation favoring women, such as quotas in election legislation to encourage women to stand as candidates for positions on local decision-making bodies, or the possible allocation of funds to municipalities conducting projects involving more women, is essential. In addition, these laws could be combined with improving the services provided by local communities to make them more attractive (IPHR 2019).

Both CSOs and activists gained expertise in the fields in which they work through many years of activity and the experience that comes with that. Academia as well as governments and other spheres of public life could benefit from this expertise. Consequently, improved cooperation and communication between CSOs and various spheres of government is essential for the development and implementation of human rights standards, their dissemination, and education on the subject. On the other hand, civil society's role should not be constrained to only addressing interested audiences or limiting the fields of operation because of harassment. Constant obstacles such as political attacks, the public debate on foreign agent laws, traditions, and legislation that limit the work of organizations and activists must be dismantled. Instead, the work of CSOs should be valued and supported by government officials. Besides this, CSOs should include representatives from different professions and worldviews in their work, and serve as moderators between them. Again, cooperation and communication between the different spheres is essential here.

5 Sustainability and Evaluation of Successful CSO Projects

Three reasons can be identified that make it difficult for CSOs to implement sustainable projects: the international donor community, national governments, and a lack of cooperation. First, the international donors in the region have their own agendas and pursue their own goals. They rarely adjust their work or requirements to local conditions, e.g., to different forms of organization and their agendas. Although CSOs in Central Asia play a crucial role in educating and disseminating knowledge on human rights, at the same time their organizational and professional structures are weak, as they lack knowledge and experience in the fields in which they work. Consequently, some organizations carry out projects that are not in fact in line with their actual agenda, simply to suit the international donors' requirements. As a result, these organizations disappear as soon as the project comes to an end. Second, national governments control the work of organizations and do not seem particularly interested in human rights education. Consequently, activists and organizations face some of the obstacles mentioned above, such as government officials interrupting their workshops, being labeled as foreign agents, or being confronted with reporting requirements that are difficult to meet. Third, there is a lack of cooperation with local authorities as projects are being implemented. Better cooperation with the authorities could improve the sustainability, durability, and quality of a project, even once donors withdraw when the agreed funding runs out. In this case, projects could be tied to the area in which the local authority works and, in this way, have longer-lasting effects (Civicus 2021).

Besides having an impact on the sustainability of their projects, this also serves as a *measurement* tool to evaluate civil society projects in Central Asian countries. To this end, different indicators, both qualitative and quantitative, are used. Qualitative indicators show, for example, possible behavioral change or a change in the mindset of the authorities and the population. Another clear indicator of success and sustainability is if a human rights project influences policymaking and results in new legislation. Additionally, some organizations use feedback from their partners and target audiences during projects to evaluate success. Quantitative indicators used by civil society activists are the number of laws introduced based on their suggestions or as a result of the pressure they exerted, e.g., with regard to gender issues or the work of municipalities (as the abovementioned example of women in municipal councils showed). The number of newly established advocacy projects is another indicator. Individual activists being released from prison is a further measure of success, as is the number of participants repeatedly registering for workshops, as it directly shows how many people can be reached. Some CSO projects also use external evaluation.

6 Recommendations

Based on the outcomes of this project, observations, and lessons learned, we will present some recommendations for actors involved in human rights education, empowerment, and knowledge dissemination in Central Asia. Our focus will be on the international donor community, Central Asian CSOs, scholars, and academia, as well as local authorities.

All of these actors have the obligation to ensure that human rights education is provided and knowledge disseminated. But, as has already been mentioned, there is a lack of knowledge and research on this subject in the region. We advise scholars and academia to focus on research into human rights in the region in cooperation with government authorities and CSOs. The latter should be involved in these efforts, especially in collecting data on human rights violations or by contributing their practical experience. The findings of these projects, in turn, should be used for human rights teaching by organizations and activists. Ensuring that teachers of the subjects relevant to human rights who can provide instruction in the local languages are qualified should be of a greater importance for the international donor community and CSOs so that more people can be reached.

To be able to disseminate knowledge and information on human rights throughout the entire region, donors should not only focus on rural regions in Central Asia. Smaller cities and villages should also be included in project plans and be systematically addressed. Civil society organizations would also be well advised to use a wider range of online communication tools to reach a wider audience and more diverse target group. An important issue to address here is the role women play in civil societies. During the workshops, the gender dimension was a crucial point. Women often lack opportunities to engage in local development, politics, or civil society. There are various reasons for this, one of them being the traditional gender roles that also apply to many highly educated women. We recommend a stronger focus on women's participation in the region. This includes legislation favoring women, such as quotas in election laws, or to encourage women to put themselves forward as candidates for positions in local decision-making bodies.

Local authorities must start promoting human rights themselves and give students in schools, for example, the opportunity to learn about the topic. A new set of teaching materials will be required to do this. Promoting human rights through local authorities will also have advantages for CSOs and donors, by increasing their space to work and educate on human rights, as well as to disseminate knowledge and information on the subject.

Another significant point of concern is the sustainability of civil society projects in the region. As mentioned above, CSOs often struggle due to inadequate organizational and professional structures, but also due to the low degree of cooperation between those involved in human rights education. Hence, the international donor community, local authorities, academia, and CSOs must all work together and establish dialog based on trust at all stages of project implementation. The needs and concerns of CSOs must be considered at every step of the way and placed at the very heart to ensure their capacity is not exceeded and projects can be implemented in a sustainable manner. To make this possible, further specialization and professionalization of CSOs is needed.

7 Conclusion

This article, which draws on the joint program between IOS Regensburg, Germany, and the OSCE Academy in Bishkek, Kyrgyzstan, and the workshops held in Bishkek in October 2021 shows the obstacles and challenges CSOs and scholars face in their work on human rights education, empowerment, and knowledge dissemination in the countries of Central Asia since the collapse of the Soviet Union. But it also highlights the opportunities. The outcomes of the discussions that took place during the workshops illustrate the sheer range of parameters included in human rights education and knowledge dissemination in the region. Both legislation on CSOs and human rights instruments, as well as the circulation of knowledge on human rights in society and the use of social media to share information show the problems the countries of Central Asia still face. Civil society organizations are dependent on funding from the international donor community. In light of this, we must ask ourselves to what extent these financial dependencies create a space in which civil society can work sustainably.

Research, material, and the teaching of human rights in Central Asia need to be adapted accordingly. Both the national and international dimensions, including national languages, the number of human rights trainers, and local contexts, must be borne in mind, especially when it comes to the development of academia and the creation and dissemination of educational material on human rights in the region. Additionally, there is a need to collect data on human rights violations in each country and make these available for teaching and education. Central Asian civil society plays an important role, too. Civil society organizations have many years of experience in the fields in which they work, making them indispensable in cooperation with local authorities and governments. At the same time, CSOs and their work should be protected by the authorities, to enable them to continue their projects without harassment, thus increasing their sustainability.

Our recommendations for those involved in human rights education and knowledge dissemination in Central Asia are addressed to the international donor community as well as CSOs, scholars, and authorities. We have developed a set of guidelines based on the outcomes and lessons learned from the project and workshops conducted with a view to improving cooperation and the sustainability of projects in the region.

References

Civicus (2021) Restrictive "false" information and NGO laws adopted, intimidation of government critics. https://monitor.civicus.org/updates/2021/09/20/restrictive-false-information-and-ngo-laws-adopted-intimidation-government-critics/. Accessed 8 Sept 2022

Civicus (2022) Continued Repression under New President. https://monitor.civicus.org/updates/2022/07/27/continued-repression-under-new-president/. Accessed 8 Sept 2022

Diamond L (1994) Rethinking civil society: toward democratic consolidation. J Democr 5(3):4–17

Freedom House (2021a) Freedom in the World 2021. https://freedomhouse.org/country/uzbekistan/freedom-world/2021. Accessed 8 Sept 2022

HRW: Human Rights Watch (2020a) Uzbekistan–Events of 2020. https://www.hrw.org/world-report/2021/country-chapters/uzbekistan. Accessed 13 Septr 2022

HRW: Human Rights Watch (2020b) Turkmenistan–Events of 2020. https://www.hrw.org/world-report/2021/country-chapters/turkmenistan. Accessed 13 Sept 2022

IPHR: International Partnership for Human Rights (2019) Joint NGO submission to the United Nations Human Rights Committee ahead of the consideration of Tajikistan's Third Periodic Report at the 126th session in July 2019. Torture, ill-treatment, the death penalty and the shrinking space for NGOs. June 2019. https://www.iphronline.org/wp-content/uploads/2019/06/Tajikistan-torture-submission-1.pdf. Accessed 3 Sept 2022

IPHR: International Partnership for Human Rights (2021a) Kyrgyzstan update: Restrictive "false" info and NGO laws adopted, intimidation of government critics. https://www.iphronline.org/kyrgyzstan-update-restrictive-false-info-and-ngo-laws-adopted-intimidation-of-government-critics.html. Accessed 3 Sept 2022

IPHR: International Partnership for Human Rights (2021b) No space for criticism: Excessive restrictions on fundamental freedoms across Central Asia. https://www.iphronline.org/wp-content/uploads/2021/11/Joint-no-space-for-criticism-paper-November-2021.pdf. Accessed 10 Sept 2022

IPHR: International Partnership for Human Rights (2021c) Tajikistan: Torture and ill-treatment, human rights violations in the armed forces, death penalty, domestic violence, LGBT, persons with disabilities, freedom of association. https://www.iphronline.org/wp-content/uploads/2021/09/UPR-Taj-torture.pdf. Accessed 13 Sept 2022

IPHR: International Partnership for Human Rights (2021d) Uzbekistan-Key human rights concerns and individual cases. https://www.iphronline.org/eu-uzbekistan-human-rights-dialogue-2021.html. Accessed 13 Sept 2022

Smith A (2019) Civic Space under threat across Central Asia, Russia and Eastern Europe

Transparency International/International Partnership for Human Rights (2021) Closed civic space in Turkmenistan. Widening crackdown on dissent. https://www.iphronline.org/wp-content/uploads/2021/06/CLOSED-CIVIC-SPACE-IN-TURKMENISTAN-JUNE-2021-1.pdf. Accessed 11 Sept 2022

UN Special Rapporteur on Human Rights Defenders (2022) Kyrgyzstan: amendments to Law on Non-Commercial Organizations may impinge on exercise of rights to freedom of expression and freedom of association (joint communication). https://srdefenders.org/kyrgyzstan-amendments-to-law-on-non-commercial-organizations-ncos-may-impinge-on-exercise-of-rights-to-freedom-of-expression-and-freedom-of-association-joint-communication/. Accessed 13 Sept 2022

University Overview: Accessed 9 Sept 2022. Kazahkstan: https://kls.kazguu.kz/en/, https://www.kimep.kz/school-of-law/en/, https://yur.enu.kz, https://www.kaznu.kz/en/357/page/%20Departments/Law_Faculty, http://kriu.edu.kz/en/department/department-of-training-law/; Tajikistan: www.rtsu.tj, https://tnu.tj/wp-content/uploads/2020/09/faculty-of-law.pdf, http://tsulbp.tj/glavnaya; Turkmenistan: https://www.mfa.gov.tm/en/articles/51?breadcrumbs=no, https://www.tdu.edu.tm/?/Faculty%20of%20Law/&page=19&in=69, https://iuhd.edu.tm/faculty/4; Uzbekistan: https://www.uwed.uz/en/faculties/international-law, https://tsul.uz/uz/general-page/Faculty%20of%20Law-QS, www.samdu.uz

Open Access This chapter is licensed under the terms of the Creative Commons Attribution 4.0 International License (http://creativecommons.org/licenses/by/4.0/), which permits use, sharing, adaptation, distribution and reproduction in any medium or format, as long as you give appropriate credit to the original author(s) and the source, provide a link to the Creative Commons license and indicate if changes were made.

The images or other third party material in this chapter are included in the chapter's Creative Commons license, unless indicated otherwise in a credit line to the material. If material is not included in the chapter's Creative Commons license and your intended use is not permitted by statutory regulation or exceeds the permitted use, you will need to obtain permission directly from the copyright holder.

Human Rights in Central Asia - Challenges and Perspectives

Sergey Sayapin

1 Introduction

Now that I have written this chapter, I realize that it was an exercise in the relativity of law and legal sociology. The chapter is about "human rights", but its limited scope compelled me to mention some and omit others. The focus is on civil and political rights, although economic, social, and cultural rights are also dealt with. The chapter is about "Central Asia", but the truth is that there is no single Central Asia, and not only do the Central Asian states—Kazakhstan, Kyrgyzstan, Tajikistan, Turkmenistan, and Uzbekistan—differ from one other but each also displays important internal differences. Such differences—for example, competition for power between regional clans[1]—inform regular political processes within the states but on a few occasions have resulted in situations of violence. The Central Asian states have acceded to all the major instruments of international human rights law but when it comes to implementation, much work remains to be done, in particular, as far as the freedom of the press, rule of law, independence of the judiciary, corruption perception, and gender inequality are concerned. The constitutions of all Central Asian states contain provisions about the democratic character of their respective political regimes[2] but politicians across the region often insist that democratic practices in the region are

---

[1] See: Collins (2003).

[2] Cf. Article 1(1) of the Constitution of the Republic of Kazakhstan, Article 1(1) of the Constitution of the Kyrgyz Republic, Article 1 of the Constitution of the Republic of Tajikistan, Article 1 of the Constitution of Turkmenistan, and Article 1 of the Constitution of the Republic of Uzbekistan.

This chapter is an updated version of Sayapin 2022, Copyright 2022 by Routledge. Reproduced by permission of Taylor & Francis Group.

S. Sayapin (✉)
School of Law, KIMEP University, Almaty, Kazakhstan
e-mail: s.sayapin@kimep.kz

© The Author(s) 2023
A. Mihr and C. Wittke (eds.), *Human Rights Dissemination in Central Asia*,
SpringerBriefs in Political Science,
https://doi.org/10.1007/978-3-031-27972-0_2

"unique", and some incidents interpreted by the West as human rights violations merely testify to local peculiarities that can be justified by cultural relativism.[3]

Most of the human rights issues that persist in Central Asia are, at least in part, attributable to the Soviet past. Central Asia's key policymakers came from the Soviet nomenclature, and it is unsurprising that the evolution of the political rhetoric about democracy (of which human rights are a constituent element) in post-Soviet Central Asia comprised three stages: "(1) decisive statements about the course toward democracy at the beginning of independence; (2) statements about the possibility of an exclusively national model of democracy; (3) recognition of enlightened authoritarianism as the most suitable fundament for the political system".[4] Overcoming this Soviet legacy is a matter of political evolution, and requires time and political will. Instead of formally listing the instruments of international human rights law which the individual Central Asian states have acceded to, this chapter highlights some of the most critical human rights issues, along with some of the most notable achievements in each country, in order to exemplify the regional human rights dynamics since 1991. It is hoped that the interdisciplinary methodology employed will place human rights in the broader sociological context they deserve, and illustrate their relationship with political, economic, and other developments in post-Soviet Central Asia. General observations and recommendations are offered in the Concluding Remarks section.

2 Kazakhstan

An economic leader in the region,[5] Kazakhstan also positions itself as a regional political power with a multi-vector foreign policy.[6] Since 1991, it has been trying to balance its development priorities with other commitments, including international human rights law, with varying degrees of success. In 1993, the Bolashak International Scholarship was established to help talented Kazakhstani youth obtain world-class higher education abroad. In the same year, a highly efficient human rights NGO—the Kazakhstan International Bureau for Human Rights and Rule of Law—was established. The Soros Foundation Kazakhstan has been supporting human rights initiatives in the country since 1995. A moratorium on the death penalty has been in place since 1 January 2004,[7] and in 2020, Kazakhstan acceded to the Second Optional Protocol to the International Covenant on Civil and Political Rights (ICCPR) and abolished the death penalty in accordance with its provisions.[8] In 2013, a National

---

[3] Alston and Goodman (2013), pp. 531–681.
[4] Tolipov (2007), p. 7.
[5] According to the World Bank, in 2020, Kazakhstan's GDP was 159.8 billion USD. For comparison, the GDP of Central Asia's second largest economy, Uzbekistan, was 57.7 billion USD.
[6] Zhussupova (2021).
[7] Adilet (2003).
[8] Radio Azattyq (2021a).

Preventive Mechanism (NPM) was put in place to prevent and eliminate torture and other forms of ill-treatment. Since the annexation of Crimea in 2014, the government introduced a program of voluntary resettlement of ethnic Kazakhs from the south to the north of the country,[9] and several Kazakh nationals were sentenced under Article 172 of the Criminal Code for taking part in the ongoing armed conflict in eastern Ukraine.[10] Anti-corruption reforms included the establishment of an efficient system of e-government (Egov) and a network of public service centers (TSON). Legislation on trade unions was amended in 2020. According to Human Rights Watch, "[t]he most notable change is the removal of a requirement that local and industrial tier trade unions must affiliate with a higher tier trade union body or risk losing their right to legally carry out any activities, a violation of the right of trade unions to freely determine their structure [...] Other positive changes include simplified registration requirements and an extension from 6 to 12 months to complete registration procedures. The amendments make it clear in law that trade unions in Kazakhstan have the right to join international trade union organizations, and to jointly organize events and projects with them".[11] On the other hand, a number of issues have attracted the attention of domestic and international human rights monitors. As of this writing, one individual complaint had been considered under the Optional Protocol to the Convention on the Elimination of All Forms of Discrimination against Women, 15 individual complaints had been submitted under the Convention against Torture, and 45 individual complaints had been considered under the First Optional Protocol to the ICCPR.[12] On 16–17 December 2011, police used force against protesters in Zhanaozen, as a result of which 17 people were killed and more than a hundred were wounded, according to official data.[13] Domestic violence is widespread and sexual violence, including against children, is a continuing issue.[14] To respond to the latter problem, in 2019 and 2020, criminal responsibility for sexual crimes was reinforced (cf. Articles 120–124 of the Criminal Code).

After the first President of Kazakhstan Nursultan Nazarbayev resigned on 19 March 2019, Kassym-Jomart Tokayev was elected to the post on 9 June 2019, which heralded a number of human rights reforms. In particular, the concept of a "listening state" was announced with a view to improving the quality of dialogue with civil society,[15] legislation on peaceful assemblies was revised,[16] and, in 2021, the electoral law was reformed.[17] In 2019, the Ministry of Justice initiated amendments to the Law

---

[9] Kovaleva (2018).

[10] For the text of the Criminal Code (in Russian), see: https://online.zakon.kz/document/?doc_id=31575252 (last accessed 7 August 2022).

[11] Human Rights Watch (2020a).

[12] For data, see: https://tbinternet.ohchr.org/_layouts/15/TreatyBodyExternal/Countries.aspx?CountryCode=KAZ&Lang=EN (last accessed 7 August 2022).

[13] Radio Azattyq (2020).

[14] Human Rights Watch (2019a).

[15] Strategy 2050 (2020).

[16] International Commission of Jurists (2020).

[17] The Astana Times (2021).

on Advocacy and Legal Aid, which, according to some commentators, might cause substantial harm to the independence of legal advisers[18] and make legal services more expensive.[19] On 12 May 2021, President Tokayev requested that the Constitutional Council assess the compatibility of the proposed amendments to the Constitution of Kazakhstan.[20] On 4 June 2021, the Constitutional Council found a "lack of clarity and inconsistency of some of [the proposed] provisions with related norms, which [might] create conditions for their ambiguous understanding and improper application".[21] At the same time, however, the Council ruled that the amendments were compatible with the Constitution.[22] Despite the controversy, the amendments were adopted on 9 June 2021.

3 Kyrgyzstan

Kyrgyzstan is a paradoxical nation. Often referred to as Central Asia's "island of democracy",[23] Kyrgyzstan experienced two revolutions (in 2005 and 2010), which suggests that the political system's ability to facilitate a peaceful transition of power is limited, albeit in a way that differs from its neighbors. The country's political landscape has been dominated by competition for power between the "north" and the "south" ever since 1991.[24] Organized crime is yet another serious factor.[25] Kyrgyzstan retains a strong Soviet legacy—statues of Lenin, Marx, and Engels can still be seen in the center of Bishkek, and Kyrgyzstan has an active communist party. Russia retains strong influence over politics, the economy, military affairs, and higher education: Kyrgyzstan is a member of the Eurasian Economic Union (EAEU, joined in 2015), it hosts a joint Russian military base,[26] and the Kyrgyz-Russian Slavonic University (KRSU) was established as early as 1992. At the same time, Kyrgyzstan's higher education offering includes the American University of Central Asia (AUCA, founded in 1993) and the OSCE Academy in Bishkek (founded in 2002). Until 2021, non-governmental organizations (NGOs), including local and international human rights NGOs, could operate relatively freely.

---

[18] Alyokhova (2020).

[19] Galiyev and Sayapin (2020).

[20] Alyokhova (2021).

[21] See: Regulatory Resolution No. 1 of the Constitutional Council of the Republic of Kazakhstan, dated 4 June 2021 On checking for compliance with the Constitution of the Republic of Kazakhstan the Law of the Republic of Kazakhstan On Amendments and Additions to Certain Legislative Acts of the Republic of Kazakhstan on Advocacy and Legal Assistance, para. 6.

[22] *Ibid.*, para. 5.

[23] See *passim* Anderson (1999).

[24] Radio Azattyq (2010).

[25] Radio Azattyq (2019).

[26] In 2001–2014, there was also a US military base at the Manas international airport near Bishkek.

At the time of writing, one individual complaint had been submitted against Kyrgyzstan under the Optional Protocol to the Convention on the Elimination of All Forms of Discrimination against Women, and the Human Rights Committee had considered no fewer than 43 individual complaints under the First Optional Protocol to the ICCPR.[27] Violence against women and girls is widespread.[28] Although explicitly proscribed by Article 175 of the Criminal Code,[29] bride kidnapping remains a pressing issue.[30] Massive inter-ethnic violence, which erupted in the south of the country in June 2010,[31] and likely amounted to crimes against humanity,[32] has still not been fully investigated. Kyrgyzstan included the concept of crimes against humanity in its Criminal Code in 2016—the only Central Asian state to have done so.[33] A prominent human rights defender, ethnic Uzbek Azimjon Askarov, who had been working on the documentation of the violent events in 2010 was given a life sentence and died in prison on 25 July 2020.[34]

Since 1991, Kyrgyzstan has enacted three Constitutions—in 1993, 2010, and, most recently, in 2021. The 1993 Constitution was amended on several occasions with a view to reinforcing the authority of the president.[35] After Presidents Askar Akayev and Kurmanbek Bakiyev had been ousted from office, *inter alia*, on the grounds of corruption and abuse of power, the 2010 Constitution replaced the presidential republic with a parliamentary one.[36] The most recent Constitution was enacted on 5 May 2021.[37] It consolidated the power of the president in that it transferred "power from the parliament to the president to appoint members of the cabinet, and appoint and dismiss judges, the prosecutor general, the chairman of the national bank, and members of the Accounting Chamber, as well as nominate and dismiss half of the Central Election Committee, undermining their independence from the executive".[38] The new Constitution also placed restrictions on the rights to freedom of expression, assembly, and association, and introduced new regulations for NGOs and political parties.[39] It remains to be seen where this worrying trend will take the country.

---

[27] For data, see: https://tbinternet.ohchr.org/_layouts/15/TreatyBodyExternal/Countries.aspx?CountryCode=KGZ&Lang=EN (last accessed 7 August 2022).

[28] Human Rights Watch (2019b).

[29] For the text of the Criminal Code (in Russian), see: https://online.zakon.kz/document/?doc_id=34350840 (last accessed 7 August 2022).

[30] Human Rights Watch (2021a); the problem also persists in Kazakhstan, see: Isa (2020).

[31] Human Rights Watch (2010).

[32] Amnesty International (2011).

[33] Sayapin (2020a), pp.130–134.

[34] Human Rights Watch (2021b).

[35] For the text of the 1993 Constitution (in Russian), see: https://online.zakon.kz/document/?doc_id=30212746#pos=4;-108 (last accessed 7 August 2022).

[36] For the text of the 2010 Constitution (in Russian), see: http://cbd.minjust.gov.kg/act/view/ru-ru/202913 (last accessed 7 August 2022).

[37] For the text of the 2021 Constitution (in Russian), see: http://cbd.minjust.gov.kg/act/view/ru-ru/112215 (last accessed 7 August 2022).

[38] Human Rights Watch (2021c).

[39] *Ibid.*

4 Tajikistan

Complicated by religion, competition for power among regional clans, social traditions, and the enduring legacy of the violent non-international armed conflict that took place in 1992–1997,[40] the human rights situation in Tajikistan is quite tense.[41] Domestic violence is widespread[42] and early marriages occur.[43] Arbitrary detentions of opposition supporters[44] and attacks against journalists[45] have been recorded. The situation is exacerbated by the weakness of Tajikistan's economy[46]: in 2019, personal remittances received by families of Tajik labor migrants working abroad (primarily, in the Russian Federation) constituted 28.6 percent of the overall GDP.[47] Like in Kyrgyzstan, Russia's influence in the politics, military affairs, and education space of Tajikistan is extensive. Tajikistan hosts Russia's 201st military base (at the time of writing, Russia's military presence in the country has been confirmed until 2042), is a member of the Collective Security Treaty Organization (CSTO),[48] and the Tajik President Emomali Rakhmon—who had been in power since 1994 and appointed his elder son as mayor of Tajikistan's capital Dushanbe in 2017[49]—was the only foreign head of state present at the annual victory parade in Moscow in 2021.[50] The Russian-Tajik Slavonic University (RTSU) was founded in 1996 and is one of the most popular higher education institutions in Tajikistan. In 2020–2021, Russia reportedly invested up to 30 million USD in the construction of Russian schools in Tajikistan.[51] According to Article 2 of the Constitution of Tajikistan, Russian is the "language of inter-ethnic communication".[52] With all these factors in place, Russian influence is going to be around for decades to come.

As of this writing, the Human Rights Committee had considered no fewer than 29 individual complaints under the First Optional Protocol to the ICCPR.[53] The COVID-19 pandemic posed a serious challenge to Tajikistan, as it did to the other Central Asian states, including in terms of respect for human rights. Tajikistan did

---

[40] Atadjanov (2021).
[41] Human Rights Watch (2021d).
[42] Human Rights Watch (2019c).
[43] UNFPA (2014).
[44] Human Rights Watch (2020b).
[45] Human Rights Watch (2020c).
[46] According to the World Bank, in 2019, Tajikistan's GDP was 8.1 billion USD, and GDP per capita was 874 USD.
[47] World Bank (2019).
[48] In Central Asia, Kazakhstan and Kyrgyzstan are also members of the CSTO. See: Sayapin (2021).
[49] BBC News (2017).
[50] Khurshudyan (2021).
[51] SNG.Today (2020).
[52] For the text of the Constitution of the Republic of Tajikistan (in Russian), see: https://online.zakon.kz/document/?doc_id=30391383 (last accessed 7 August 2022).
[53] See data at: https://tbinternet.ohchr.org/_layouts/15/TreatyBodyExternal/Countries.aspx?CountryCode=TJK&Lang=EN (last accessed 7 August 2022).

Human Rights in Central Asia - Challenges and Perspectives   21

not acknowledge the existence of COVID-19 cases on its territory until 30 April 2020.[54] According to Human Rights Watch, "Tajik authorities have provided some information about how to prevent the spread of Covid-19 on government ministry websites, and have visited some schools, universities, and army bases to inform people about the disease".[55] Still, "they have not imposed a quarantine or encouraged social distancing in any meaningful way. The government did not cancel Nowruz, or New Year, festivities in late March, and schools, businesses, and most public spaces remain[ed] open".[56] Obviously, above and beyond the right to the highest attainable standard of health, throughout Central Asia, the COVID-19 pandemic affected, *inter alia*, the right to education at all levels, access to justice, as well as the rights to freedom of movement, expression, and assembly.[57]

5 Turkmenistan

Turkmenistan is the most complex Central Asian nation. The authoritarian political system is rigidly controlled by the president, and independent human rights scrutiny is very difficult.[58] In 1985, Saparmurat Niyazov became First Secretary of the Turkmen Communist Party and remained in power as the first President of Turkmenistan (*Türkmenbaşy*—"Head of the Turkmen") until his death in December 2006. Turkmenistan became a permanently neutral state in 1995,[59] and maintains conscription-based armed forces.[60] During Niyazov's time in power, opera, ballet, and circuses were banned (in 2001), the months of the year and weekdays were renamed (in 2002), and his two-volume book, *Ruhnama*, became mandatory reading at all schools, higher education institutions, and government agencies. The information the book contained was required to qualify for a driver's license, and quotes from *Ruhnama*, along with those from the Quran, were built into the walls of the Türkmenbaşy Ruhy Mosque in Turkmenistan's capital city Ashgabat. Niyazov's successor, Gurbanguly Berdimuhamedow, also had sweeping powers in the largely isolated political system and held the title of *Arkadag* ("Protector"). Berdimuhamedow published no fewer than 55 books on various subjects,[61] some of which people "worship[ped] like bread or the Quran, kissing them upon receipt and applying the coveted tome to their foreheads".[62] Meanwhile, the mass media are strictly censored, access to the internet is

---

[54] Radio Free Europe—Radio Liberty (2020).
[55] Human Rights Watch (2020d).
[56] *Ibid.*
[57] *Ibid.*
[58] Human Rights Watch (2021e).
[59] See: Constitutional Law of Turkmenistan on Permanent Neutrality of Turkmenistan, https://www.refworld.org/pdfid/405ab3d14.pdf (last accessed 7 August 2022).
[60] World Bank (2018).
[61] Hronika (2020).
[62] Polovinko (2020).

limited, and political dissent is suppressed.[63] Gurbanguly Berdimuhamedow's only son Serdar was a member of parliament, held a few posts in the executive, was appointed Deputy Chairman of the Cabinet of Ministers on 11 February 2021,[64] and was elected third President of Turkmenistan on 12 March 2022.

The social and economic situation in the country is difficult. As of June 2021, Turkmenistan has not reported a single COVID-19 case,[65] but in July 2020, the World Health Organization (WHO) already advised the Turkmen authorities to take "critical public health measures [...] as if COVID-19 was circulating". On 3 June 2021, the Union Cycliste Internationale (UCI) announced that the 2021 Tissot UCI Track Cycling World Championships, which were scheduled to take place in Ashgabat on 13–17 October 2021, "have been cancelled in their initial format, at the request of their organisers, as the health constraints and restrictions linked to the Covid-19 pandemic make it impossible to stage the event in the country".[66] Earlier in 2021, food queues were banned, "in order not to discredit the president".[67] As of this writing, the Human Rights Committee had considered no fewer than 23 individual complaints under the First Optional Protocol to the ICCPR.[68] The fact that the other Central Asian countries' statistics are higher can only be due to practical obstacles in communicating the Turkmen cases to the Human Rights Committee and other human rights bodies.

6 Uzbekistan

Although the Universal Declaration of Human Rights was the first international legal instrument ratified by Uzbekistan after proclaiming its independence on 31 August 1991,[69] the human rights record of post-Soviet Uzbekistan remained consistently problematic until 2016—indeed, Human Rights Watch referred to it as "abysmal".[70] The powers of the Ministry of Interior and the National Security Service were sweeping, and a Law on Internal Affairs Bodies was not adopted until 2016,[71] with the National Security Service being reorganized into the State Security Service in

---

[63] Human Rights Watch (2021e).

[64] Radio Azattyq (2021b).

[65] Fergana Agency (2021).

[66] UCI (2021).

[67] Radio Azattyq (2021c). According to the World Bank, in 2018, Turkmenistan's GDP was 40.76 billion USD, and GDP per capita was 6,966 USD.

[68] See data at: https://tbinternet.ohchr.org/_layouts/15/TreatyBodyExternal/Countries.aspx?CountryCode=TKM&Lang=EN (last accessed 7 August 2022).

[69] The Universal Declaration of Human Rights is not a treaty but the sovereign Uzbekistan did formally ratify the Declaration on 30 September 1991. See: Mustaqillik (1991).

[70] Human Rights Watch (2021f).

[71] See the text of the Law (in Russian): https://lex.uz/docs/3027845 (last accessed 7 August 2022).

2018.[72] As of this writing, one individual complaint had been submitted against Uzbekistan under the Convention against Torture, and the Human Rights Committee had considered no fewer than 53 individual complaints under the First Optional Protocol to the ICCPR.[73] According to the former UN Special Rapporteur on Torture, Theo van Boven, torture in Uzbek places of detention was "systematic" at the time of his visit to the country in 2002.[74] The name "Zhaslyk"—a detention facility in the west of the country—became synonymous with ill-treatment. The second President of Uzbekistan, Shavkat Mirziyoyev, ordered Zhaslyk's closure in 2019.[75] On 13 May 2005, a protest in the eastern Uzbek town of Andijan was suppressed,[76] and strict measures against civil society and foreign and international organizations represented in Uzbekistan followed.[77] The death penalty was abolished as of 1 January 2008.[78] According to the International Labour Organization (ILO), the use of forced labor, including child labor, in the cotton harvest was "systematic and systemic" in the country, until a report issued in early 2021 confirmed that "[s]ystematic child labour has been eradicated and child labour [was] no longer a major concern".[79] According to the same report, "[t]he Uzbek government has significantly increased wages since 2017 and introduced a differentiated pay scale so that pickers are paid more per kilogramme of cotton towards the end of the harvest, when conditions are less favourable and there is less cotton to pick. This has led to a significant drop in the prevalence of forced labour".[80] The government has also recognized the issue of labor migration,[81] and started taking measures to improve the situation of labor migrants abroad.[82]

Progressive reforms carried out in Uzbekistan since 2016 are bearing fruit. The number of acquittals in criminal cases has increased significantly since 2017.[83] In 2018, President Mirziyoyev mandated a revision of the Criminal and Criminal Procedure Codes of Uzbekistan, among other things, with a view to filling "gaps in criminal law and procedure resulting in inadequate protection of human rights and freedoms".[84] Although the draft of a new edition of Uzbekistan's Criminal Code does

---

[72] See the Law On the State Security Service of the Republic of Uzbekistan (in Russian) at: https://www.lex.uz/docs/3610937 (last accessed 7 August 2022).

[73] See data at: https://tbinternet.ohchr.org/_layouts/15/TreatyBodyExternal/Countries.aspx?CountryCode=UZB&Lang=EN (last accessed 7 August 2022).

[74] Eshanova (2002).

[75] Gazeta.Uz (2019).

[76] Human Rights Watch (2005).

[77] Al Jazeera (2015).

[78] See Decree No. UP-3641 On the Abolition of the Death Penalty in the Republic of Uzbekistan of 1 August 2005 (in Russian) at: https://lex.uz/docs/1264449 (last accessed 7 August 2022).

[79] International Labour Organization (2021).

[80] *Ibid*.

[81] Radio Free Europe–Radio Liberty (2013).

[82] IWPR Central Asia (2021).

[83] Sayapin (2019a), p. 22; Sayapin (2019b), p. 662.

[84] Sayapin (2020b), p. 37.

contain a few notable improvements, it has also attracted some criticism on the part of international human rights experts, in particular, in the context of offenses related to the exercise of the freedom of association, domestic violence, LGBT rights, and criticism of public figures.[85] Uzbekistan is cooperating with expert organizations—such as the International Commission of Jurists—on the implementation of international law, in particular, on economic, social, and cultural rights, as well as access to justice.[86] On 21 December 2019, *The Economist* opined that "no other country has advanced that far", and named Uzbekistan "country of the year".[87] In early 2020, Uzbekistan announced the completion of mine clearance along its border with Tajikistan. Given that over the past 20 years, a total of 374 citizens of Tajikistan had been killed by anti-personnel landmines, and another 485 Tajik nationals injured,[88] the humanitarian significance of this development is outstanding. On 22 June 2020, the President of Uzbekistan approved a National Human Rights Strategy of the Republic of Uzbekistan,[89] which expounds, on 66 pages, the functions of various national authorities with respect to the implementation of international human rights law and recommends measures on human rights education.

7 Concluding Remarks

Thirty years after the dissolution of the Soviet Union, the Central Asian states are still learning to apply international human rights law, and to communicate about it with external and domestic audiences. Most recently, the COVID-19 pandemic exposed numerous issues with the region's implementation of human rights in practice, and not only with respect to healthcare per se. Access to information was not always consistent, the statistical methods employed were at times contradictory, the legal status of regulations issued by the "Chief Sanitary Doctors" was uncertain, and the legal challenges posed by the state of emergency regime were considerable.[90] The transition to online education was not a satisfactory solution, in terms of quality, for larger families which lacked the hardware to allow their children to all attend classes simultaneously.[91] Defense lawyers reported that online—civil but, especially, administrative and criminal—trials via WhatsApp were not a good solution either, among other things, due to the limited number of participants in a session and difficulties

---

[85] Human Rights Watch (2021g).
[86] International Commission of Jurists (2021).
[87] The Economist (2019).
[88] The Tashkent Times (2020).
[89] See Decree No. UP-6012 On Approval of the National Strategy of the Republic of Uzbekistan on Human Rights of 22 June 2020 (in Russian) at: https://lex.uz/ru/docs/4872357 (last accessed 7 August 2022).
[90] Human Rights Watch (2020d).
[91] Otyrar.Kz (2020).

related to the examination of evidence.[92] The consequences of these ad hoc solutions are yet to be seen. But there are also useful lessons to be learnt.

Central Asian governments should invest, as a matter of urgency, in the digitalization of administrative procedures, and other public services. Doing so will increase the efficiency and speed of such procedures, significantly reduce the risk of corruption, and visibly improve the quality of dialogue between governments and civil society. Instead of introducing new rules, regulatory barriers should be taken down, wherever possible, especially in the field of the economy. There should be greater transparency and accountability in political decision-making. Such reforms would help modernize economic and political systems and improve the quality of life of the region's populations.

Due to the region's political culture, workable reforms will only come from the top. This means, in effect, that governments should recognize that compliance with international human rights law is not "harmful" to the state, but in fact will ultimately contribute to "further strengthening the country's authority in the international arena, in particular, improving the position [of the state] in economic, political and legal rankings and indices".[93] International human rights are closely linked to all areas of life, and respect for human rights is an important indicator both for international investors and policymakers,[94] as it testifies to the stability, predictability, and trustworthiness of a state's judiciary and law enforcement system. Judges—especially those dealing with criminal and administrative cases—and law enforcement officers should be trained on the application of domestic and international human rights law, and states should genuinely align their law enforcement practices with their obligations under the applicable human rights instruments. Importantly, international human rights treaties and constitutional provisions on human rights should be directly applicable in domestic legal systems. Decisive measures must be taken to combat torture and other forms of ill-treatment. The legal status and influence of national human rights institutions should be raised,[95] and they should be staffed by individuals with professional knowledge of international human rights law, international humanitarian law, and international criminal law. Regular dialogue with the UN human rights organs, as well as international and domestic human rights NGOs would be helpful. The cumulative effect of such measures will benefit individuals, society, and the government alike.

---

[92] Informburo.Kz (2020).

[93] See *supra* note 88, 4th preambular paragraph.

[94] It is worth noting here that the Enhanced Partnership and Cooperation Agreement between the European Union and its Member States, on the one hand, and the Republic of Kazakhstan, on the other, adopted on 21 December 2015, explicitly mentions "human rights" on at least 20 occasions. For the text of the Agreement, see: https://eur-lex.europa.eu/legal-content/EN/TXT/PDF/?uri=CELEX:22016A0204(01)&from=EN (last accessed 7 August 2022).

[95] OHCHR (2021).

References

Adilet (2003) О введении в Республике Казахстан моратория на смертную казнь [On the Introduction of a Moratorium on the Death Penalty in the Republic of Kazakhstan]. https://adilet.zan.kz/rus/docs/T030001251. Accessed 7 Aug 2022

Fergana Agency (2021) Ашхабад отказался принять чемпионат мира-2021 по велотреку [Ashgabat Refuses to Host the 2021 Track Cycling Championship]. https://fergana.agency/news/122194/. Accessed 7 Aug 2022.

Alston P, Goodman R (2013) International human rights: text and materials. Oxford University Press, Oxford

Alyokhova A (2020) Новый "налог" от Минюста: коррупционные риски и лазейки [A New "Tax" from the Ministry of Justice: Corruption Risks and Loopholes]. https://365info.kz/2020/12/novyj-nalog-ot-minyusta-korruptsionnye-riski-i-lazejki. Accessed 7 Aug 2022

Alyokhova A (2021) Обращение Токаева в Конституционный совет по закону о юристах – беспрецедентный случай [Tokayev's Reference to the Constitutional Council Regarding the Law on Lawyers is an Unprecedented Case]. https://365info.kz/2021/05/obrashhenie-tokaeva-v-konstitutsionnyj-sovet-po-zakonu-o-yuristah-bespretsedentnyj-sluchaj. Accessed 7 Aug 2022

Amnesty International (2011) Kyrgyzstan Must Deliver Justice to Victims of Crimes against Humanity. https://www.amnestyusa.org/press-releases/kyrgyzstan-must-deliver-justice-to-victims-of-crimes-against-humanity-2-2/. Accessed 7 Aug 2022

Anderson J (1999) Kyrgyzstan: central Asia's island of democracy? Routledge, Abington

Atadjanov R (2021) Non-international armed conflict in Tajikistan. In: Lee et al (eds) Encyclopedia of public international law in Asia, Volume III: Central & South Asia. Brill, Leiden, pp 207–208

Radio Azattyq (2010) Традиционное деление Кыргызстана на Север и Юг проходит экзамен на единство нации [The Traditional Division of Kyrgyzstan into North and South Passes the Test for the Unity of the Nation]. https://rus.azattyq.org/a/kyrgyzstan_north_south/2030369.html. Accessed 7 Aug 2022

Radio Azattyq (2012) "Дом пыток", откуда нет обратного пути ["The House of Torture" from Where There is No Way Back]. https://rus.azattyq.org/a/jaslyk-prison-of-uzbekistan-torture/24670352.html. Accessed 7 Aug 2022

Radio Azattyq (2019) Борьба с организованной преступностью в КР: на чьей стороне перевес? [Fighting Organized Crime in the Kyrgyz Republic: Who Will Prevail?]. https://rus.azattyk.org/a/kyrgyzstan_crime_security/29918622.html. Accessed 7 Aug 2022

Radio Azattyq (2020) Жанаозен. Незаживающая рана [Zhanaozen—An Unhealing Wound]. https://rus.azattyq.org/a/kazakhstan-zhanaozen-2011-documentary-azattyq-12162020/31002595.html. Accessed 7 Aug 2022

Radio Azattyq (2021a) Токаев подписал закон об отмене смертной казни [Tokayev Signs a Law Abolishing the Death Penalty]. https://rus.azattyq.org/a/31030302.html. Accessed 7 Aug 2022

Radio Azattyq (2021b) Очевидный наследник? Как президент Туркменистана готовит сына к власти [The Obvious Heir? How the President of Turkmenistan is Preparing his Son for Power]. https://rus.azattyq.org/a/31106981.html. Accessed 7 Aug 2022

Radio Azattyq (2021c) В Туркменистане запретили очереди за продуктами, чтобы не дискредитировать президента [Turkmenistan Banned Food Queues in Order not to Discredit the President]. https://rus.azattyq.org/a/31227843.html. Accessed 7 Aug 2022

Collins K (2003) The political role of clans in central Asia. Comp Polit 35:171–190

The Economist (2019) Which nation improved the most in 2019?. https://www.economist.com/leaders/2019/12/21/which-nation-improved-the-most-in-2019. Accessed 7 Aug 2022

Eshanova Z (2002) Uzbekistan: UN rapporteur says use of torture "Systematic". https://www.rferl.org/a/1101615.html. Accessed 7 Aug 2022

Radio Free Europe–Radio Liberty (2013) Karimov: Uzbek Migrants Are "Lazy", Beggars Don't Exist. https://www.rferl.org/a/uzbekistan-karimov-beggars-migrants-remittances/25028531.html. Accessed 7 Aug 2022

Radio Free Europe–Radio Liberty (2020) COVID-19: Tajikistan officially confirms first cases. https://www.rferl.org/a/covid-19-kyrgyzstan-easing-business-restrictions/30585076.html. Accessed 7 Aug 2022

Galiyev N, Sayapin S (2020) О цене доступа к профессии [On the Cost of Access to the Profession]. https://online.zakon.kz/m/Document/?doc_id=34509671&fbclid=IwAR0K4euTSid=34509671&fbclid=IwAR0K4euTSAlLq6hwc1S5zbDfYkAlLq6hwc1S5zbDfYk--7KWmdUns3EJ5VXGlgdctEGcBc6mRNdro7KWmdUns3EJ5VXGlgdctEGcBc6mRNdro. Accessed 7 Aug 2022

Gazeta Uz (2019) Колония "Жаслык" ликвидируется – постановление президента [Zhaslyk Colony to be Wound Up by the President's Regulation]. https://www.gazeta.uz/ru/2019/08/03/jaslyk/. Accessed 7 Aug 2022

Hronika TM (2020) Бердымухамедов написал книгу про нейтралитет Туркменистана [Berdimuhamedow Writes Book about the Neutrality of Turkmenistan]. https://www.hronikatm.com/2020/12/neutrality-book/. Accessed 7 Aug 2022

Human Rights Watch (2005) "Bullets Were Falling like Rain": The Andijan Massacre, May 13, 2005. https://www.hrw.org/report/2005/06/06/bullets-were-falling-rain/andijan-massacre-may-13-2005. Accessed 7 Aug 2022

Human Rights Watch (2010) Where is the justice?. https://www.hrw.org/report/2010/08/16/where-justice/interethnic-violence-southern-kyrgyzstan-and-its-aftermath. Accessed 7 Aug 2022

Human Rights Watch (2019a) Kazakhstan: little help for domestic violence survivors. https://www.hrw.org/news/2019/10/17/kazakhstan-little-help-domestic-violence-survivors. Accessed 7 Aug 2022

Human Rights Watch (2019b) Kyrgyzstan: pressure builds to protect women and girls. https://www.hrw.org/news/2019/05/28/kyrgyzstan-pressure-builds-protect-women-and-girls. Accessed 7 Aug 2022

Human Rights Watch (2019c) Tajikistan: barriers to aid for domestic violence victims. https://www.hrw.org/news/2019/09/19/tajikistan-barriers-aid-domestic-violence-victims. Accessed 7 Aug 2022

Human Rights Watch (2020a) Kazakhstan adopts long-promised amendments to trade union law. https://www.hrw.org/news/2020/12/17/kazakhstan-adopts-long-promised-amendments-trade-union-law. Accessed 7 Aug 2022

Human Rights Watch (2020b) Tajikistan: intensified pressure on dissidents' families. https://www.hrw.org/news/2020/07/09/tajikistan-intensified-pressure-dissidents-families. Accessed 7 Aug 2022

Human Rights Watch (2020c) Attack on Tajik Journalist Reporting on Covid-19. https://www.hrw.org/news/2020/05/13/attack-tajik-journalist-reporting-covid-19. Accessed 7 Aug 2022

Human Rights Watch (2020d) Central Asia: respect rights in Covid-19 responses. https://www.hrw.org/news/2020/04/23/central-asia-respect-rights-covid-19-responses. Accessed 7 Aug 2022

Human Rights Watch (2021a) Another woman killed in scourge of Kyrgyzstan: "Bride Kidnappings". https://www.hrw.org/news/2021/04/09/another-woman-killed-scourge-kyrgyzstan-bride-kidnappings. Accessed 7 Aug 2022

Human Rights Watch (2021b) Documentary calls for justice for Kyrgyzstan's Azimjon Askarov. https://www.hrw.org/news/2021/06/02/documentary-calls-justice-kyrgyzstans-azimjon-askarov. Accessed 7 Aug 2022

Human Rights Watch (2021c) Kyrgyzstan: withdraw problematic draft constitution. https://www.hrw.org/news/2021/03/05/kyrgyzstan-withdraw-problematic-draft-constitution. Accessed 7 Aug 2022

Human Rights Watch (2021d) Tajikistan. https://www.hrw.org/europe/central-asia/tajikistan. Accessed 7 Aug 2022

Human Rights Watch (2021e) Turkmenistan. https://www.hrw.org/europe/central-asia/turkmenistan. Accessed 7 Aug 2022.

Human Rights Watch (2021f) Uzbekistan. https://www.hrw.org/europe/central-asia/uzbekistan. Accessed 7 Aug 2022

Human Rights Watch (2021g) Uzbekistan: draft criminal code offers little meaningful reform. https://www.hrw.org/news/2021/03/10/uzbekistan-draft-criminal-code-offers-little-meaningful-reform. Accessed 7 Aug 2022

Informburo.Kz (2020) В Казахстане суды проходят онлайн. Не нарушает ли это закон и права казахстанцев? [In Kazakhstan, Trials are Held Online. Does this not Violate the Law and the Rights of Kazakhstanis?]. https://informburo.kz/stati/v-kazahstane-sudy-prohodyat-onlayn-ne-narushaet-li-eto-zakon-i-prava-kazahstancev.html. Accessed 7 Aug 2022

International Commission of Jurists (2020) Kazakhstan: draft law on peaceful assemblies should be reconsidered. https://www.icj.org/kazakhstan-draft-law-on-peaceful-assemblies-should-be-reconsidered/. Accessed 7 Aug 2022

International Commission of Jurists (2021) Region and country archives: Uzbekistan. https://www.icj.org/country/europe/uzbekistan/. Accessed 7 Aug 2022

International Labour Organization (2021) Systemic forced labour and child labour has come to an end in Uzbek cotton. https://www.ilo.org/washington/news/WCMS_767753/lang--en/index.htm. Accessed 7 Aug 2022

Isa D (2020) "Не хотела запятнать честь отца": истории похищенных невест ["I Didn't Want to Tarnish my Father's Honour": Stories of Abducted Brides]. https://rus.azattyq.org/a/kazakhstan-brobe-kidnapping/30466749.html. Accessed 7 Aug 2022

IWPR Central Asia (2021) Uzbekistan Looks to diversify labour migration. https://iwpr.net/global-voices/uzbekistan-looks-diversify-labour-migration. Accessed 7 Aug 2022

Al Jazeera (2015) Uzbekistan: 10 years after the Andjian massacre. https://www.aljazeera.com/features/2015/5/12/uzbekistan-10-years-after-the-andijan-massacre. Accessed 7 Aug 2022

Khurshudyan I (2021) At Russia's Victory Day parade, a show of military might amid tensions with the West. https://www.washingtonpost.com/photography/interactive/2021/russia-parade-victory-day-putin/. Accessed 7 Aug 2022

Kovaleva I (2018) С юга на север. Как работает программа переселения? [From South to North. How does the Resettlement Program Work?]. https://vlast.kz/obsshestvo/30742-s-ugana-sever-kak-rabotaet-programma-pereselenia.html. Accessed 7 Aug 2022

Mustaqillik (1991) Республика Узбекистан ратифицировала всеобщую декларацию прав человека [The Republic of Uzbekistan Ratifies the Universal Declaration of Human Rights]. http://mustaqillik.uz/ru/events/view/83. Accessed 7 Aug 2022

BBC News (2017) Сын главы Таджикистана назначен мэром Душанбе [The Son of the Head of Tajikistan is Appointed Mayor of Dushanbe]. https://www.bbc.com/russian/news-38598174. Accessed 7 Aug. 2022

OHCHR (2021) UN human rights and NHRIs. https://www.ohchr.org/en/countries/nhri/pages/nhrimain.aspx. Accessed 7 Aug 2022

Otyrar.Kz (2020) О трудностях дистанционного обучения рассказали многодетные семьи [Large Families Talk about the Difficulties of Distance Learning]. https://otyrar.kz/2020/07/o-trudnostyah-distantsionnogo-obucheniya-rasskazali-mnogodetnye-semi/. Accessed 7 Aug 2022

Polovinko V (2020) Аркадаг и Океания [Arkadag and Oceania]. https://novayagazeta.ru/articles/2020/08/07/86567-argadag-i-okeaniya. Accessed 7 Aug 2022

Reuters (2020) WHO urges Turkmenistan to take steps "as if COVID-19 was circulating". https://www.reuters.com/article/us-health-coronavirus-turkmenistan-idUSKCN24G276. Accessed 7 Aug 2022

Sayapin S (2019a) "Critical Analysis, Strict Discipline and Personal Responsibility": Some reflections on strengthening the independence of the judiciary in Central Asia. Law State 3(84):18–27

Sayapin S (2019b) Réflexions sur le renforcement de l'indépendance de la magistrature en Asie centrale [Reflections on the Reinforcement of the Independence of the Judiciary in Central Asia]. Les Cahiers De La Justice 14:655–665

Sayapin S (2020a) Why a crimes against humanity convention from a perspective of post-soviet states? African J Int Criminal Justice 6:125–135

Sayapin S (2020b) Crimes against the peace and security of mankind in the revised edition of the criminal code of the Republic of Uzbekistan. Rev Central East Euro Law 45:36–58

Sayapin S (2021) Collective Security Treaty Organisation (CSTO). In: Lee et al (ed) Encyclopedia of public international law in Asia, Volume III: Central & South Asia. Brill, Leiden, pp 184–185

Sayapin S (2022) Human rights in post-soviet central Asia. In: Leontiev L, Amarasinghe P (eds) State-building, rule of law, good governance and human rights in post-soviet space. Routledge, Abington, pp 135–149

Strategy 2050 (2020) Концепция "Слышащее государство": от слов к действию [The Concept of a "Listening State": From Words to Action]. https://strategy2050.kz/ru/news/kontseptsiya-slyshashchee-gosudarstvo-ot-slov-k-deystviyu/. Accessed 7 Aug 2022

The Astana Times (2021) New law on elections aims to engage Kazakh Citizens in political institutions, experts say. https://astanatimes.com/2021/05/new-law-on-elections-aims-to-engage-kazakh-citizens-in-political-institutions-experts-say/. Accessed 7 Aug 2022

The Tashkent Times (2020) Uzbekistan completes mine clearance of its border with Tajikistan. https://tashkenttimes.uz/national/4816-uzbekistan-completes-mine-clearance-of-its-border-with-tajikistan. Accessed 7 Aug 2022

SNG.Today (2020) Россия потратит $30 млн на строительство русских школ в Таджикистане [Russia will Spend 30 million USD on the Construction of Russian Schools in Tajikistan]. https://sng.today/dushanbe/15330-rossija-potratit-30-mln-na-stroitelstvo-russkih-shkol-v-tadzhikistane.html. Accessed 7 Aug 2022

Tolipov F (2007) Государства Центральной Азии: универсальная демократия, национальная демократия или просвещенный авторитаризм? [Central Asian States: Universal Democracy, National Democracy, or Enlightened Authoritarianism?]. Central Asia Caucasus 2(50):7–19

UCI (2021) UCI statement concerning the 2021 Tissot UCI track cycling world championships. https://www.uci.org/inside-uci/press-releases/uci-statement-concerning-the-2021-tissot-uci-track-cycling-world-championships. Accessed 7 Aug 2022

UNFPA (2014) Child Marriage in Tajikistan (Overview). https://eeca.unfpa.org/sites/default/files/pub-pdf/unfpa%20tajikistan%20overview.pdf. Accessed 7 Aug 2022

World Bank (2018) Armed forces personnel, total–Turkmenistan. https://data.worldbank.org/indicator/MS.MIL.TOTL.P1?locations=TM. Accessed 7 Aug 2022

World Bank (2019) Personal remittances, received (% of GDP)–Tajikistan. https://data.worldbank.org/indicator/BX.TRF.PWKR.DT.GD.ZS?locations=TJ. Accessed 7 Aug 2022

Zhussupova A (2021) Peace through engagement: the multi-vector direction of Kazakhstan's Foreign policy. https://astanatimes.com/2021/03/peace-through-engagement-the-multi-vector-direction-of-kazakhstans-foreign-policy/. Accessed 7 Aug 2022

Open Access This chapter is licensed under the terms of the Creative Commons Attribution 4.0 International License (http://creativecommons.org/licenses/by/4.0/), which permits use, sharing, adaptation, distribution and reproduction in any medium or format, as long as you give appropriate credit to the original author(s) and the source, provide a link to the Creative Commons license and indicate if changes were made.

The images or other third party material in this chapter are included in the chapter's Creative Commons license, unless indicated otherwise in a credit line to the material. If material is not included in the chapter's Creative Commons license and your intended use is not permitted by statutory regulation or exceeds the permitted use, you will need to obtain permission directly from the copyright holder.

Human Rights Education in Central Asia

Anja Mihr

1 Introduction

The 2011 United Nations Declaration on Human Rights Education and Training (HRET) describes human rights education (HRE) as a tool that:

> promotes values, beliefs, and attitudes that encourage all individuals to uphold their rights and those of others. It develops an understanding of everyone's common responsibility to make human rights a reality in each community.
>
> (UN Declaration on Human Rights Education and Training 2011)

Human rights are universally and internationally agreed norms and standards that are guaranteed legally and politically and are enshrined in international human rights law (IHRL), which has been in practice since the establishment of the UN Charter in 1945 and the Universal Declaration of Human Rights (UDHR) in 1948. All five Central Asian states—Kazakhstan, Uzbekistan, Kyrgyzstan, Tajikistan, and Turkmenistan—are members of the UN and have adhered to the UN Charter since their independence from the Soviet Union in 1991. All of them have ratified most of the core human rights treaties, and three of them (Kyrgyzstan, Kazakhstan, and Uzbekistan) have been elected to the UN Human Rights Council. The latter comply with the UN Human Rights Council's mechanisms, such as Universal Periodic Reviews and Special Procedures, albeit often reluctantly.

The UN is the key international standard-setter for human rights in Central Asia. The UN Regional Centre for Preventive Diplomacy for Central Asia (UNRCCA) and many other UN sub-branches and agencies have offices in the region. Other international players in Central Asia are the Organization for Security and Co-

A. Mihr (✉)
DAAD Professor for Human Rights, OSCE Academy, Bishkek, Kyrgyzstan
e-mail: a.mihr@osce-academy.net

© The Author(s) 2023
A. Mihr and C. Wittke (eds.), *Human Rights Dissemination in Central Asia*, SpringerBriefs in Political Science,
https://doi.org/10.1007/978-3-031-27972-0_3

operation (OSCE) and the Shanghai Cooperation Organisation (SCO).[1] All Central Asian states are members of the OSCE, which runs annual Human Rights Dialogues and summits through its Office for Democratic Institutions and Human Rights (ODIHR) to which Central Asian countries respond. The SCO has no human rights mechanism.

Another explicitly regional human rights framework is the Convention on Human Rights and Fundamental Freedoms of the Commonwealth of Independent States (CIS) established by the successor organization of the Soviet Union and in force since the early 1990s. The Convention that is driven by post-soviet states, reiterates the importance of the UDHR, the International Covenant on Economic, Social and Cultural Rights (ICESCR), the International Covenant on Civil and Political Rights (ICCPR), as well as all international obligations on human rights assumed within the OSCE to apply to Central Asian countries.[2] By becoming a party to the Convention in the 1990s, all Central Asian states formally agreed to the fundamental rights and freedoms, as enshrined in the UDHR and other international human rights treaties. However, unlike the UN treaties, the 1995 Convention on Human Rights and Fundamental Freedoms of the CIS has neither monitoring nor enforcement mechanisms and is therefore seen as obsolete. The members of the Convention's monitoring commission failed to intervene when member states violated or abused the fundamental rights and freedoms that the Convention included. The commission leaves any intervention to other international bodies, such as the ODIHR and the UN Human Rights Council.

Consequently, the only international legal framework with mechanisms for regular monitoring and enforcement, as well as support for HRE in the region, is the UN and the Office of the High Commissioner for Human Rights (OHCHR) in Geneva, and its branch in Central Asia, which is based in the capital of Kyrgyzstan, Bishkek.

1.1 Human Rights Education in Central Asia

Although none of the Central Asian governments deliberately deny or exclude themselves from the UDHR or other general human rights agreements, let alone international law and customary law, they are poorly implemented.

The same is true for HRE. Central Asian governments do not reject the different phases of the World Programme for Human Rights Education, which has been ongoing since the first UN Decade for HRE in 1994–2004. All Central Asian states endorsed the Decade in 1993 during the UN World Conference for Human Rights in Vienna. Yet, to this day, none of the regional governments has had any serious National Action Plan for HRE. Kyrgyzstan, Kazakhstan, and Uzbekistan

---

[1] Except for Turkmenistan, which is not a member of the SCO.

[2] The International Bill of Human Rights, ten core global human rights treaties. UN Office of the High Commissioner for Human Rights, The International Bill of Human Rights. Available at https://www.ohchr.org/Documents/Publications/FactSheet2Rev.1en.pdf.

have National Action Plans for human rights and sustainability, as required by the UN, but none for HRE.

Together with the UN Educational, Scientific and Cultural Organization (UNESCO) and other international organizations, the countries of Central Asia have established action plans and schemes that combine human rights and education in the formal education sector, but none that is predominantly HRE.

Human rights education is grounded in disseminating information on universal human rights norms through formal education sectors, such as state schools and universities, and private schools that apply state curricula. That said, informal sectors, that is, civil society organizations (CSOs), non-governmental organizations (NGOs), and human rights defenders (HRDs), such as lawyers, teachers, activists, and volunteers, are also a pivotal part of the fulfillment of HRE National Action Plans. Around the world, the informal sector is much more active in implementing HRE than the formal sector. The two sectors often complement each other, with NGOs also going into schools to give extracurricular courses on human rights. In most post-Soviet Central Asian countries, the key role in disseminating knowledge on and promoting human rights norms and practices is played by CSOs, NGOs, social media, and HRDs. Ministries of Education and National Action Plans that involve the formal sector are largely absent.[3] The Canadian Human Rights Foundation (CHRF), for example, trained many teachers and multipliers to become human rights educators in a project until 2005. Once funding had run dry, however, the training stopped. The CHRF project helped teachers to include human rights on the syllabus and invited CSOs to the classroom to talk about human rights (CHRF 2005), Human Rights Education in Schools in Central Asia, CHRF Central Asian Team).

University professors who have been trained abroad, mostly in Europe and the US, tackle aspects and certain conventions of international human rights law in their legal studies curricula and, if possible, during summer schools or certified courses on human rights outside the formal curricula. Such events have been organized at the American University for Central Asia and the OSCE Academy in Bishkek, Kyrgyzstan; Webster College and the University of World Economy and Diplomacy in Tashkent, Uzbekistan; and the Eurasian Humanitarian Institute in Nur Sultan, as well as the private university KIMEP in Almaty, Kazakhstan, for example.

However, the curricula of these universities are exceptions. None of the five Central Asian states has a statute of formal HRE in either primary, secondary, or higher education. However, the student's appetite for human rights and democracy studies is vastly growing in the search for answers vis-à-vis the dysfunctional political regimes in the region. In 2022, one of my students from Tajikistan wrote in an essay that "(…) the attempts of the people all over the world for living in democratic states will go on, because people want to be respected, free, valued, accepted, and heard. Unfortunately, achieving democracy requires time, unity, courage, and

---

[3] EUCAM, Civil Society in Central Asia (2018), a discussion paper by Jos Boonstra, EUCAM initiative, Centre for European Security Studies (CESS) and Tika Tsertsvadze, International Partnership for Human Rights (IPHR); Civil Society and Confidence Building in Central Asia, the Caucasus and Eastern Europe (2020), Geneva Center for Security Sector Governance (Civil society in Central Asia: What role for the European Union?).

sacrifice and in Central Asian countries, people are not courageous enough yet to ask for this change".[4] In response to this, the first postgraduate regional Master in Liberak Arts and Science program on Human Rights and Sustainability (MAHRS) for Central Asian scholars and students will only be starting in 2023 at the OSCE Academy in Bishkek and the Global Campus of Human Rights in Venice, Italy, with the support of the European Union (EU) and donor states.

2 Human Rights in Central Asia

All Central Asian countries have a poor human rights record, according to UN reports.[5] Cases of human rights violations and abuses brought to court by HRDs are often contested or rejected. Fundamental human rights, such as freedom of religion and expression and access to information, are suppressed. Moreover, grave human rights violations, such as torture and ill-treatment, are frequently reported by HRDs, but mostly to no avail.[6] Consequently, since the independence of the five post-Soviet Central Asian states in 1991, their human rights situation has constantly been under scrutiny by CSOs, NGOs, and international governmental organizations (IGOs). The UN and the UN Human Rights Council is the primary organization that monitors human rights in Central Asia, complemented by the OSCE/ODIHR and its annual Human Dimension Meetings in Warsaw until 2020. They have been suspended since 2021, and their future and installment remain open.

---

[4] Student essay on 'Good Governance and Transformation in Central Asia', OSCE Academy in Bishkek, 2022.

[5] The key normative references for HRE and the HRET Declaration is the UN World Programme for HRE and the International Bill of Human Rights. See UN World Programme for Human Rights. Available at https://www.ohchr.org/en/resources/educators/human-rights-education-training/world-programme-human-rights-education/phase4). The Bill enshrines ten key UN declarations and conventions that define and outline universal human rights norms and standards—most of which are today considered part of customary international law. Hence, even if the UN core treaties have not all been ratified by all five Central Asian states, their norms are applicable and enforceable in each of the five countries due to their customary legal status. However, whether judges and lawyers, let alone HRDs and teachers refer to them as customary is a matter of awareness and HRE. The core treaties, for example, define the human right to physical integrity and the need to abolish torture and ill-treatment, as well as to combat racism and xenophobia, to promote and protect women's and girls' rights, social, cultural, religious, and economic rights, political and civil rights, the rights of migrants. Treaties condemn disappearances and emphasize the importance of the rights of people with disabilities and the rights of children. These human rights should be seen as norms and standards. They are "tools" or "keys" to develop or "unlock" people's capacity to create a peaceful life of justice and equality in their communities. Enhancing, respecting, and enforcing human rights ought to protect us from harm in the form of ill-treatment and discrimination that could prevent us from prospering. One of these empowerment rights (Art. 26 in the UDHR) is the right to education, which allows us to develop to the best of our abilities and live a dignified life.

[6] Treaty Database on UN OHCHR. Available at https://www.un.org/en/about-us/udhr/foundation-of-international-human-rights-law (Accessed Dec 2022).

The EU, the Council of Europe (CoE), and other international development agencies conduct human rights dialogues and training and provide financial support for HRE programs in the region. In 2018, the first UN and OSCE-led Forum on Human Rights took place in Samarkand, Uzbekistan, focusing on sustainable development, economic stability, and anti-terrorism. In December 2022, for the first time, the UN Global Forum for Human Rights Education took place in Uzbekistan, joined by the EU, the CoE, and the OSCE; aiming to highlight the importance of HRE in Central Asia which has been the white spot for HRE in comparison to other regions in the world. The Forum celebrated the 10th anniversary of the Declaration on Education and Training in Human Rights.[7] The participating governments from Central Asia confirmed the need for more academic and digital programs for HRE and marginalized groups. But as human rights are a highly contested area of debate and fulfillment, it remains to be seen whether and how Central Asian governments will keep their word.

At the same time, the human rights situation in Central Asia continues to deteriorate. Achievements, such as making domestic violence more prominent on the national agenda, are often short-lived and unsustainable. This perpetual lack of human rights compliance is associated with the increasing level of dysfunctional and corrupt political leadership and democratic backsliding, undoing any democratic achievements made after 1991. Mass detentions of journalists and demonstrators or legal trials used to intimidate the possible opposition, as seen in Kazakhstan in 2022, are expensive to maintain (Lemon 2019).

While thanks to social media sites such as Facebook and messenger services such as Telegram and WhatsApp, the countries' violations and breaches of human rights have become more transparent, the polarization of anti-Western propaganda, and hence anti-human rights propaganda, has increased in recent decades. The rise of dynastic regimes in Turkmenistan and Tajikistan, the stronghold of autocracy in Uzbekistan and Kazakhstan, and the re-autocratization of Kyrgyzstan's once semi-parliamentarian regime since 2019 has beamed these countries back to the 1990s and their strictly authoritarian presidential regimes. The space for CSOs is under threat, social media tools are censored, NGOs are being expelled from the region, and access to the internet has, because of the energy crisis, become inaccessible for many due to the high costs and low quality. Radical political reforms and security laws have reduced the liberal space, media and internet freedoms, and social mobility for millions. Although access to the internet is not denied in any country, the high cost and poor quality are major obstacles. Yet, the internet remains the main tool of knowledge transfer and information for any form of HRE (Coysh 2018).

---

[7] UN Global Forum on "Education in the field of human rights". Samarkand, Uzbekistan 5–6 December 2022, https://www.un.int/uzbekistan/news/global-forum-education-field-human-rights-samarkand-december-5-6-2022 (Accessed Dec 2022).

3 Impact of Human Rights Education

Over the past few decades, we have seen dramatic democratic backsliding, increased reports on human rights violations, and a rise in populist ethnic-nationalist governments in Central Asia. The 2011 HRET Declaration, the 2015 Sustainable Development Goals (SDGs), as well as the ongoing UN World Programme for HRE, all emphasize human rights education, training, and dissemination of human rights standards as the essential tools to solve the region's critical problems and challenges, including climate change and poverty-induced migration, minority rights, corruption, women's and children's rights, and anti-terrorism measures which are often in breach of human rights norms.[8]

The 1999 UN General Comment on human rights highlights the importance of HRE not only in disseminating the idea of human rights and implementing those rights. The Comment states that HRE is a tool to promote universal norms, namely that.

> (…) education shall be directed to the human personality's sense of dignity, it shall 'enable' all persons to participate effectively in a free society, and it shall promote understanding among all 'ethnic' groups, as well as nations and racial and religious groups".[9] It also emphasizes, from a philosophical perspective, that HRE enables "(…) a well-educated, enlightened and active mind…to wander freely and widely," which it describes as "one of the joys and rewards of human existence.[10]

For HRE to have any impact on changing people's attitudes and behavior, the informal sector is pivotal. Human rights education still only reaches a self-selecting audience, namely those who consciously choose to attend training. Most of the population in the five Central Asian countries remains largely unaware of human rights and has no experience with HRE. Individual engagement, social movements, and general social media are often the only way to ensure that human rights-related knowledge, training, and capacity-building measures reach a broader, mainly younger audience. This informal space illustrates how human rights cultures emerge and evolve in social settings, often without guidance or context, and thus fail to impart an understanding of the full spectrum of human rights. The informal sector plays a pivotal role in HRE in Central Asia because the state is absent, unable, or unwilling to promote HRE in primary and secondary education.

---

[8] In its resolution 24/15 (8 October 2013), the UN Human Rights Council decided to focus the World Programme's third phase (2015–2019) on strengthening the implementation of the first two phases and promoting human rights training for media professionals and journalists. This resolution was adopted following the OHCHR consultation on the focus of the third phase, as presented in the High Commissioner's report A/HRC/24/24. The OHCHR, in consultation with States, intergovernmental organizations, national human rights institutions, and civil society elaborated a plan of action for the third phase (2015–2019) of the World Programme.

[9] UN OCHCHR (1999) CESCR General Comment No. 13: The Right to Education (Art. 13). Adopted at the Twenty-first Session of the Committee on Economic, Social and Cultural Rights, on 8 December 1999 (Contained in Document E/C.12/1999/10).

[10] *Ibid.*

The current fourth phase of the World Programme for Human Rights Education was launched in 2020. It will run until 2024, focusing on young people and their need for human rights empowerment in times of migration and urbanization. Half of the Central Asian population is under 30, a crucial target group for this phase. Many of these young people are frustrated with poor governance and the lack of social mobility and therefore seek opportunities elsewhere or risk their lives and safety protesting these conditions in Almaty (Kazakhstan), Bishkek (Kyrgyzstan), and Karakalpakstan (an autonomous republic within Uzbekistan). The number of young migrants from Central Asia who move abroad to Dubai, Russia, Turkey, and Europe is among the highest in the world.

Because of the lack of proper formal education in human rights, the volume of online and offline material used to teach and train citizens on their human rights has peaked in recent years, partly due to the COVID-19 pandemic and the need to develop more online tools. This material has increased human rights awareness but not necessarily empowerment. Article 26 of the UDHR and Articles 13 and 14 of the ICESCR underline that everyone has a fundamental right to education—at least elementary education. Education and lifelong learning should, according to these two documents, be aimed at fully developing the human personality and respect for human rights and fundamental freedoms.

However, with the increasing access to the internet and online learning, the state authorities have strengthened their surveillance, persecution, censorship, and anti-Western propaganda—blaming "Western human rights and liberties" for the shortcomings, poverty, and inequality in their countries. Instead of seeing HRE as a solution to corruption and inequality, governments oppose it. At the same time, thousands of bloggers, protesters, HRDs, and civic activists, seeking improved compliance with human rights norms have been arrested. This has made it even more difficult to integrate HRE into the formal education sector—except for subjects related to sustainability, women's and children's rights, and the environment, which are relatively undisputed and can therefore be taught more easily by NGOs and even in the classroom (Tibbitts 2020).

In Kazakhstan, for example, as stated by Yevgeny Zhovtis, head of Kazakhstan's International Bureau for Human Rights, HRE depends on the political context and leadership. Although lip service and government promises to respect universal human rights and conduct HRE have increased in the past decade, so have human rights abuses and violations. This is more disquieting considering UN Human Rights Council memberships. In 2015, Kyrgyzstan joined the UN Human Rights Council, and Kazakhstan and Uzbekistan were elected to the Council in 2021. All have emphasized their commitments to the World Programme for HRE and the SDGs. Except for Turkmenistan, all four Central Asian countries continue participating in the UN's Universal Periodic Review (UPR). Commitment at the international level is not the problem, but at the grassroots level and in the classroom, human rights are conspicuously absent.

Governments show a certain political will to respond to international trends and submit reports, but the situation is different at the local level. For example, in February 2019, Uzbek foreign minister Vladimir Norov addressed the United Nations General

Assembly (UN GA) in a letter highlighting the importance of all human rights for the development of the Central Asian Republics. In his letter, Norov summarized the results of the first UN-led Forum on Human Rights, which took place in Samarkand in November 2018, to enhance Uzbekistan's candidacy for the UN Human Rights Council.

The Forum was the first of its kind in Central Asia and part of the celebrations for the 70th anniversary of the UDHR. All Central Asian representatives reiterated their commitment to the Declaration. They stressed that international human rights treaties would continue to be the political yardstick for domestic security policies, judicial reforms, and development policy, as well as education. The governmental representatives, ombudsmen, and women, and CSOs emphasized that compliance with human rights is an internal matter, not an external one. This was considered a milestone.

Outside the conference rooms in Samarkand, the societal and political reality was different. Anti-Western and anti-human rights sentiment is on the rise throughout the region, all the more since Russia's unlawful aggression against Ukraine and the subsequent war in 2022. This will make it even more difficult for HRE to be implemented and HRDs to continue their work in the post-Soviet space in the future. The ongoing support for Russia's position on international human rights and the Soviet legacy of arbitrary and political justice is far from constituting a reputable rule of law system. The Soviet legacy has never been unpacked—from a political, historical, or legal perspective. As a glorified and unchallenged political legacy, it threatens democratization and the rule of law in all Central Asian republics. And much of this unchallenged past is reflected, not least in the nature and seriousness of human rights violations (Omelicheva 2018: 57–80). After 1991, opportunities to introduce structural legal and political reforms to democratize and establish a political environment that adheres to the rule of law were missed, as was state building. This has led to a situation where CSOs heavily depend on individual alliances with policymakers and their willingness to support HRE.

4 Samarkand Declaration 2018 for Human Rights Education

At the end of the Central Asian Human Rights Forum in November 2018, the participating states from the region and beyond signed the Samarkand Declaration. The document highlighted the importance of civil society and underlined the delegates' commitment to the SDGs and the UDHR. They also stressed the role of other quasi-non-governmental and independent domestic bodies in monitoring human rights compliance in their respective countries. This included the National Human Rights Institutes (NHRIs) and Ombudsmen institutions. Central Asian delegates emphasized the importance of an independent judiciary and private actors for the future well-being of the Central Asian republics.

Apart from these rather hollow promises, the Declaration has since been a door-opener for all non-governmental actors wanting to conduct more HRE. At the same time, however, governments have repeatedly claimed that human rights are Western and European rights and have little to do with the "traditional values" of Central Asian nations. An explanation as to exactly what these traditional values are, however, is nowhere to be found.

Nevertheless, in the Samarkand Declaration, the word "education" is mentioned 11 times, mostly in promoting general educational efforts to enhance human rights compliance. Paragraph 19, however, reads:

> For education, training and public awareness on human rights and the SDGs, States shall strive to eradicate illiteracy, to provide direct training to enable the full development of human personality and to strengthen respect for human rights and fundamental freedoms.
>
> States shall seek to enhance mutual understanding, tolerance and peace within countries and internationally.
>
> In this regard, states should include human rights, humanitarian law, democracy, development and social justice, development and recommendations against food waste in the curricula of all institutions of formal and informal education. States shall enhance human rights education covering all strata of the population, including all categories of civil servants, judiciary, law enforcement, local self-government officials and civil society representatives.
>
> States shall include human rights education, including on women's rights, SDGs and electoral rights, into formal and informal educational programmes.[11]

If any regions' governments were to adhere to anything they had signed, they would have to incorporate HRE in all aspects of the formal and informal education sector. Since 2018, however, nothing of that sort has happened, and even at the 2022 Global Forum for HRE in Samarkand, little or nothing was said about the implementation and progress of the 2018 Declaration. Nevertheless, Central Asian governments are under enormous domestic pressure to deliver their promises to their younger generation by leaders of marginalized and vulnerable groups, let alone the rising middle class, striving for more social mobility and economic and political freedoms. One of the big challenges for all regional actors is how to fight the corruption and nepotism which blocks any form of serious political reform.

Despite the government's relentless emphasis on human rights, education, and compliance, the Samarkand Declaration allows CSOs and policymakers to refer to it when confronting corrupt and despotic public authorities. Yet, in paragraph 12 of the Samarkand Declaration, the signatory states emphasize that democratic mechanisms, such as an independent judiciary and a free civil society, are needed to achieve the objectives of the SDGs. For this, they must comply with all the fundamental human rights treaties that have already been ratified.

Another regional phenomenon that runs counter to the Samarkand Declaration is what has been referred to as the "re-traditionalization" of women in line with the "traditional values" of Central Asian nations promoted by the region's governments. This value rhetoric largely relates to the way women must behave, not men. As

---

[11] Samarkand Declaration 2018, UN GA Seventy-third session, 4 February 2019, Permanent Mission of Uzbekistan to the United Nations addressed to the UN Secretary-General.

a result, it strengthens the region's patriarchal societies and reverts to daughters, wives, and mothers taking on the role of housekeepers and child bearers. Another development is the rise of Muslim religious schools (known as Madrassas) for the poor. The religious charity organizations linked to these schools are often the only ones to care for the underprivileged population in Central Asia. This phenomenon has fostered a toxic mix of alleged "traditions", including bride kidnapping, keeping girls at home, and only sending boys to school. The re-emergence of the Muslim faith filled the vacuum in ideological guidance left by the collapse of the Soviet Union and allowed religious activities, suppressed for decades, to be carried out in public again. Madrassas and Muslim charity organizations have changed the paradigms and social attitudes in the region over the past three decades. Some communities have returned to pre-Russian and pre-Soviet habits and customs of not allowing girls to study or work, sending their sons to religious schools to become Imams, and fighting against corrupt state institutions. Governments across the region have responded to this rise with strict anti-terrorism measures targeting Muslim fighters, which often breach human rights. At the same time, however, regional governments are often seen entering into collaborative joint ventures with Muslim leaders, introducing state-controlled schools for Imams and building mosques while calling for a new national Central Asian Islam or a new political Islam.

Ethnic, language, and gender-related minority rights are sensitive issues in Central Asia, and the region has a poor track record when it comes to respecting and enforcing them. Violence against women is rising, and ethnic, religious, or sexual minorities are treated as scapegoats for the lack of social development. Most HRE programs focus on women's and children's rights, as these areas are less contested in the context of patriarchal structures and politics. Quite the opposite is the case if educators attempt to tackle the rights of LGBTIQs and members of ethnic minorities or other religious and language groups.[12] If at all, these rights are usually almost exclusively addressed via social media and messenger platforms, and often only in English rather than Russian or the national Central Asian languages to make the work less accessible to a wider audience and protect those HRDs who report misconduct in these groups.

It is important to stress that the pressure to improve human rights compliance and legal reforms comes from the people within these countries, not from other countries or international NGOs. Domestic and local CSOs are increasingly organized on social platforms, focusing on international human rights standards, and exchanging messages and reports via WhatsApp, Telegram, and Facebook (Abdusalyamova 2015). The continuing exodus of young people and economic dependence on third countries are increasing the pressure on governments to respond to this issue if they do not want to lose their small but well-educated class of young elites (Sharifzoda 2019).

Yet, Central Asia's brain drain continues and largely prevents investment, innovation, and the development of economies that currently remain heavily dependent on remittances. It weakens the international position of Central Asian governments vis-à-vis the surrounding hegemons, namely Russia, China, and Turkey, on which they

---

[12] Lesbian, gay, bisexual, transgender, intersex, and queer people.

are highly dependent (Pomfret 2019: 31). None of these countries has a good track record when it comes to human rights compliance, and hence place little pressure on the Central Asian governments to comply with human rights standards. The less the countries develop, economically and socially, the weaker they remain vis-à-vis their allies. In essence, this was something the 2018 Samarkand Declaration indirectly admitted and emphasized.

5 Central Asian' Human Rights (Education) Defenders

Human rights education remains in the hands of CSOs, NGOs, and higher education institutions with strong international partnerships. Without the involvement of international organizations, NGOs, and private donors, there would be no HRE programs or projects in Central Asia.[13] The UN has long relied on this political reality in Central Asia—and elsewhere—when it called for CSOs and social media to play a specific role in increasing human rights awareness and engaging in the fourth World Programme for HRE.[14]

The fact that Uzbekistan, Kyrgyzstan, and Kazakhstan have deliberately campaigned to be elected to the UN Human Rights Council and submitted their UPR illustrates their desperate need for international recognition—even if that means supporting the World Programme for HRE. They also allowed the UN, OSCE, and EU observers into the country to monitor and help support legal reforms according to international norms. Furthermore, Central Asian governments have intensified their collaboration with the Shanghai Cooperation Organization (SCO) and the Eurasian Economic Union (EAEU), showing the political will to make concessions on regional and global norms beyond their national borders. The decades since 2000 can largely be described as a transition from "nation-building"—which failed in almost all five states—to "nation finding".

Turkmenistan and Tajikistan are increasing their restrictive human rights policies and politics, even though domestically and internationally, pressure on all countries is growing. After the withdrawal of the International Security Assistance Force (ISAF) from Afghanistan in 2021 and the subsequent outbreak of civil war and the Russian war in Ukraine in 2022, isolation from the international community is the least these countries can afford. However, the gradual opening to the international arena has yet to necessarily be followed by the opening to CSOs domestically. Quite the opposite. Suppression and expulsion of NGOs and HRDs are still the norms rather than the exception, with the sole purpose of not losing control over the minds and actions of citizens. Governments in Central Asia are fully aware that the more they engage internationally and allow international companies, businesses, educators, and CSOs to operate domestically, the more people's attitudes and habits will change,

---

[13] https://www.ohchr.org/en/issues/education/training/pages/undhreducationtraining.aspx.
[14] UN Declaration on Human Rights Education and Training, GA, December 2011. Available at https://www.ohchr.org/en/issues/education/training/pages/undhreducationtraining.aspx.

sometimes in opposition to the oppressive political regimes. Hence, governments need to make concessions internationally and domestically at the same time.

One way of doing this was to become a member of the UN Human Rights Council and collaborate with the OSCE, SCO, and the EU. The EU Initiative for Human Rights and Rule of Law in Central Asia established in 2020, for example, has been endorsed by Kazakhstan and Tajikistan. Both states are under enormous pressure—internally from their own citizens and externally from countries such as Afghanistan, Russia, and China. They need international alliances to withstand these pressures.[15] The concessions they made toward the EU and the UN include a willingness to accept appropriate criticism in the form of recommendations from the UN, legal training from the EU, and compliance with policy reforms proposed by the OSCE. Uzbekistan, Kyrgyzstan, and Kazakhstan have also been voluntarily participating in the UPRs and Special Procedures of the Human Rights Council for more than ten years and recently engaged in the EU Rule of Law Initiative for Central Asia, along with the 2019 EU Central Asia Strategy.[16]

Of all the five republics, Turkmenistan is the least active when it comes to reporting on human rights and is also the country with one of the worst human rights records in the world. Independent NGOs and media do not exist, and the country is also virtually closed to independent scrutiny. An independent investigation of alleged human rights abuse is therefore impossible. Most reports on labor camps and mass violations come from the diaspora community or satellite pictures of concentration camps.

By contrast, Kyrgyzstan and Kazakhstan have tried their hardest to comply formally by submitting reports. Numerous reports have been submitted to the special UN committees on specific human rights issues, for example—albeit irregularly. The same applies to governmental reports on human rights submitted to the OSCE-ODIHR and during the ODIHR's annual Human Dimension Implementation Meeting in Warsaw.[17]

In 2008, the UN was finally allowed to establish its first regional office in Central Asia, in Bishkek. These regional headquarters cover all five countries. The main tasks of the office include advice and training of civil servants and the judiciary and, if requested by the government, training of law enforcement personnel or public

---

[15] All country reports pertaining to the human rights treaties, UPRs, and Special Procedures for the Central Asian countries can be found on the UN OHCHR database. Available at https://www.ohchr.org/en/publicationsresources/pages/databases.aspx (accessed January 2022).

[16] The UN human rights treaties are: UN Convention against Torture and Other Cruel, Inhuman or Degrading Treatment or Punishment; International Covenant on Civil and Political Rights (ICCPR); International Convention for the Protection of All Persons from Enforced Disappearance (ICPPED); Convention on the Elimination of All Forms of Discrimination Against Women (CEDAW); International Convention on the Elimination of All Forms of Racial Discrimination (CERD); International Covenant on Economic, Social and Cultural Rights (ICESCR); International Convention on the Protection of the Rights of All Migrant Workers and Members of Their Families (CRMW); Convention on the Rights of the Child (CRC); Convention on the Rights of Persons with Disabilities (CRPD).

[17] OSCE-ODIHR, Annual Human Dimension Implementation Meetings. Available at https://www.osce.org/odihr/hdim.

servants (OHCHR, Annual Report 2018). The office also supports national human rights institutions in the region and helps build civil society. It is actively campaigning for the deployment of UN Special Rapporteurs on discrimination, torture, independence of the judiciary, detention conditions, HIV, and domestic violence. These activities had previously just been part of the Central Asian countries' foreign policies and are now gradually becoming part of domestic policies (Omelicheva and Markowitz 2019).

The Kyrgyz government was one of the first to convene a Human Rights Coordination Council in 2013, for example. However, it adopted an action plan for implementing freedoms in December 2019 in response to UN demands (Kabar 2019). Kazakhstan, Kyrgyzstan, and Uzbekistan also took part in earlier EU Human Rights Dialogues from 2008 onward. Yet, all these activities have been, for the most part, isolated projects and programs, often in the run-up to an international meeting. All countries still need to incorporate HRE and legal reforms into their formal education and public sector, which would lead to sustainable change and compliance with human rights norms.

6 Conclusion

Human rights education in Central Asia started in the early 2000s as teachers being trained by some international NGOs with the aim of human rights becoming a school subject—something which never materialized, however. Human rights education began as an informal, private matter between a few educated elites but soon developed into activists campaigning and increasing the number of HRDs. Through CSOs, activists, and social media, HRE has proactively changed minds, attitudes, habits, and behavior across the region. That said, it has never been shaped by proper professional educational guidance. As a result, for many, human rights often remain an obscure set of norms that are not easy to apply because their purpose is not understood.

Approximately 90% of all activities, programs, and training are conducted by CSOs, NGOs, and HRDs, and are supported by the UN and its sub-agencies, as well as the OSCE and the EU. As in other parts of the world, in the five Central Asian countries, too, CSOs are the primary actors and agents of HRE—such as it exists. They achieve this with support and funding from the UN, EU, OSCE, and other private international donors, such as the Open Society Foundation, political and philanthropic foundations, the German Agency for International Cooperation (GIZ), Japanese and Canadian development grants, and USAID. Without funding from these organizations for trainers, there would be no HRE.

As a result, human rights awareness is often incomplete and biased. This can sometimes lead to the resentment of one group of people toward another, for example, men against women, Muslims against Christians, LGBTIQ against ethnic minorities, and so on. Sometimes, therefore, it can lead to more breaches of human rights norms than reconciliation. Thus, the desire for full control over education is not only a legacy of the Soviet period but also a fundamental claim of authoritarian leadership.

The latter, however, is unable and unwilling to govern the gradual incorporation of HRE into the formal and informal education and training sectors.

References

Abdusalyamova L (2015) NGOs in Central Asia. Alliance. https://www.alliancemagazine.org/feature/ngos-in-central-asia/
Brysk A (2018) The future of human rights. Polity Press
CHRF (2005) Human rights education in schools in Central Asia. CHRF Central Asian Team
Coysh J (2018) Human rights education and the politics of knowledge. Routledge Research in Human Rights Law
Fischlin D, Nadorfy M (2007) The concise guide to global human rights. Black Rose Books
Flowers N (2015) The global movement for human rights education. Radic Teach, J Theory Pract Teach
International Justice Resource Center: Regional Systems: https://ijrcenter.org/regional/
Kabar (2019) Ensuring human rights and freedom is one of the main development goals of country; Coordination Council on Human Rights under the Government of the Kyrgyz Republic. *Kabar*. http://kabar.kg/eng/news/ensuring-human-rights-and-freedoms-is-one-of-main-development-goals-of-country-kyrgyz-deputy-pm/
Lemon Ed (ed) (2019) Critical approaches to security in Central Asia, Central Asia studies. Routledge, London
Macedo S (2006) Universal jurisdiction: national courts and the prosecution. University of Pennsylvania Press
Mihr A (2009) Human rights awareness, education and democratization: the challenge for the 21st century. J Hum Rights 8(2):177–189
Mihr A (2015) Why holocaust education is not always human rights education. J Hum Rights 16(4):525–544
Mihr A, Gibney M (eds) (2014) Handbook of human rights, 2nd volume. SAGE Publishing, London
Mihr A (2010) Human rights education. In: Denemark (ed) The international studies compendium project. Wiley-Blackwell Publishing, Oxford University Press, pp 3,439–3,456
Mihr A (2019) 'Glocal' Public Policy in Times of Global Migration. In: Grimm (ed.) Public policy in the global South. Springer Publishing VS, pp 43–66
Moses D, Duranti M, Burke R (eds) (2020) Decolonization, self-determination, and the rise of global human rights politics. Cambridge University Press
Oberleitner G (2013) Global human rights institutions. Wiley Publishers
Office of the High Commissioner for Human Rights (OHCHR) (2018) OHCHR Human Rights Council Working Group on the Universal Periodic Review, 30. /HRC/WG.6/30/TKM/1
Omelicheva MY, Markowitz LP (2019) Webs of corruption, trafficking and terrorism in Central Asia. Columbia University Press, New York
Omelicheva MY (2018) Human rights and governance in Central Asia. In: Burghart D, Daniel L, Sabonis-Helf T (eds) Central Asia in the era of sovereignty, the return of Tamerlane? Lexington Books, London, pp 57–80
Pereira W (1997) Inhuman rights: the western system and global human rights abuse. Other Indian Press
Pomfret R (2019) The Central Asian economies in the twenty-first century, paving a new silk road. Princeton University Press, Princeton
Sharifzoda K (2019) To Russia or Turkey? A Central Asian Migrant Worker's Big Choice. The Diplomat. https://thediplomat.com/2019/01/to-russia-or-turkey-a-central-asian-migrant-workers-big-choice/.

Sundrijo D (2020) Regionalizing global human rights norms in Southeast Asia. Springer International Publishers

Tibbitts F (2020) Deliberative democratic decision making, universal values, and cultural pluralism: A proposed contribution to the prevention of violent extremism through education. Prospect: Q Rev Comp Educ 48(1):79–94

UN OCHCHR, General Comments (1999) CESCR General Comment No. 13: The Right to Education (Art. 13) Adopted at the Twenty-first Session of the Committee on Economic, Social and Cultural Rights, on 8 December 1999 (Contained in Document E/C.12/1999/10)

Zajda J (ed) (2020) Human rights education globally. Springer Publishers

Relevant Websites

Human Rights Education Associates (HREA): https://hrea.org/

UN Declaration on Human Rights Education and Training, GA, December 2011: https://www.ohchr.org/en/issues/education/training/pages/undhreducationtraining.aspx

OHCHR Database: https://www.ohchr.org/EN/HRBodies/Pages/TreatyBodies.aspx

UN OHCHR: https://www.un.org/en/about-us/udhr/foundation-of-international-human-rights-law

World Programme (document A/HRC/27/28): http://www.ohchr.org/EN/Issues/Education/Training/WPHRE/ThirdPhase/Pages/ThirdPhaseIndex.aspx

Open Access This chapter is licensed under the terms of the Creative Commons Attribution 4.0 International License (http://creativecommons.org/licenses/by/4.0/), which permits use, sharing, adaptation, distribution and reproduction in any medium or format, as long as you give appropriate credit to the original author(s) and the source, provide a link to the Creative Commons license and indicate if changes were made.

The images or other third party material in this chapter are included in the chapter's Creative Commons license, unless indicated otherwise in a credit line to the material. If material is not included in the chapter's Creative Commons license and your intended use is not permitted by statutory regulation or exceeds the permitted use, you will need to obtain permission directly from the copyright holder.

Human Rights as a Concept of Public Law: Challenges for Central Asian Higher Education Systems

Rustam Atadjanov

1 Introduction

The human rights agenda in public discourse, including on the matter of dissemination of knowledge on and implementation of international human rights law (IHRL) has only gained in importance and relevance in the twenty-first century. Given the ongoing developments in the world, such as emergency situations (e.g., the COVID-19 outbreak in 2019), situations of violent conflict in 2022, and armed conflicts including Russia's war against Ukraine, the attention on and demand for human rights law and protection is not surprising. Sadly, these developments create or contribute to conditions that are conducive to violations of various human rights, above all, individual rights. The concept of human rights is often perceived as a public, moral, political, international, and/or diplomatic one. We should not forget, however, that human rights have a legal dimension, too. They are directly affected by law and human rights, in turn, affect legal concepts, norms, and principles. Hence, a proper dissemination of knowledge on and education in human rights in any political system needs to always take the legal dimension into account. In Central Asia, the dissemination of knowledge on human rights (law) through teaching and instruction has experienced many bumps along the road, and will likely continue to do so.

It is important, therefore, to look at the legal dimension of human rights and how it relates to key public law concepts, such as rule of law, civil society, and the *Rechtsstaat* and to review the role of human rights education and knowledge dissemination in raising legal awareness and promoting legal culture among the population, a particularly relevant problem for the Central Asian countries. This chapter conducts a brief analysis of the relationship between human rights and law as such. Hence, this

---

R. Atadjanov (✉)
Assistant Professor of Public and International Law, Associate Dean, KIMEP University School of Law, Almaty, Kazakhstan
e-mail: rustamatadjanov1@gmail.com

© The Author(s) 2023
A. Mihr and C. Wittke (eds.), *Human Rights Dissemination in Central Asia*, SpringerBriefs in Political Science,
https://doi.org/10.1007/978-3-031-27972-0_4

chapter will examine human rights predominantly from the perspective of its legal dimensions. It subsequently looks at the education systems of four Central Asian states, in particular, law universities and/or faculties, with a view to establishing how exactly knowledge on human rights is conveyed and taught to students in these countries. Their curricula were used if publicly available. Challenges to providing effective human rights education are reviewed, along with regional contextual factors of cultural, social, historical, economic, and political nature contributing to those challenges. Understanding such factors clearly facilitates the development of potentially useful suggestions to address said challenges, something this chapter also seeks to do. Lastly, the chapter argues in favor of applying a systemic, principled, as well as contextualized approach to improving human rights education efforts in the region.

2 Human Rights as a Concept of (Public) Law and Knowledge Dissemination

From the second half of the twentieth century onward, the concept of human rights became a permanent part of the way we think about relations between nations.[1] In the Central Asian states, this only began to be the case following their independence from the Soviet Union in 1991. Their domestic constitutions included most civil and political rights, as well as some economic, social, and cultural rights. The notion of constitutional rights also started to gain hold in the region. Moreover, human rights began to enter official and informal discourses in domestic and foreign policies of Central Asian states.

According to D'Amato, international human rights are now a legislative condition of foreign aid, they have been institutionalized in bureaucratic structures, and, perhaps most importantly, they have been indelibly stamped on the minds of the public as one of the most important standards by which to measure other countries' political systems.[2] This has continued to hold true for the first two decades of this century as well. The expression "international human rights" has a powerful emotional connotation. Arguably, "human rights" has become one of the most popular and widely used terms in the mass media's coverage of external policy issues and the conduct of states at domestic, regional, and international levels.

It is important to stress at this point that human rights also have a strong legal dimension. There are several key factors that justify this statement. First of all, human rights are provided, ensured, and guaranteed by law, i.e., by way of application of legal norms and principles; they are within and not outside the legal realm. Human rights are developed and protected using legal means. Human rights are, *inter alia*, what makes the law more than just a regulatory framework, turning a legal regime into

---

[1] Anthony D'Amato, "The Concept of Human Rights in International Law", *Columbia Law Review*, Oct., 1982, Vol. 82, No. 6 (Oct., 1982), pp. 1110–1159, at 1110.

[2] Anthony D'Amato, "The Concept of Human Rights in International Law", *Columbia Law Review*, Oct., 1982, Vol. 82, No. 6 (Oct., 1982), pp. 1110–1159, at 1110.

a system of protection. Within the human rights narrative, human rights advocates have identified the promise of "using the law as a means of social change based on a commitment to humanitarian values on a global scale."[3] This has also been true for Central Asian contexts, although the perception of and application of the law—as merely a statist tool for achieving narrow goals of ruling elites—in these countries has often created and continues to create obstacles to fulfilling that commitment.

Second, supremacy of human rights and freedoms constitute one of the fundamental features of the concept of the *Rechtsstaat* or the "state of law."[4] This aspect of democracy involves both the rights and interests of individuals and rights and freedoms of citizens.[5] In a true *Rechtsstaat*, individuals have the right to freedom in social and political life. Such a "state of law" fully recognizes this individual freedom and does not allow itself to interfere with it.[6] It is imperative that the supremacy of human rights and freedoms is not just expressed as a nominal recognition and establishment in domestic legislation on the fundamental rights and freedoms of individuals; it must actually be guaranteed in reality, with a tangible way of enforcing and fulfilling those rights, interests, and freedoms.[7] Moreover, not only are human rights and their supremacy one of the key features of the idea of the *Rechtsstaat*, they also act as one of the preconditions for the establishment of a true "state of law"; in other words where there is no respect for human rights, there will also be no chance of a *Rechtsstaat* or "state of law" in any form.

Third, the "legal culture" element is also important. This could be defined as a network of values and attitudes relating to law, which determines why, where, and when people turn to (or turn away from) the law or the government. As lawyers are well aware, legal culture encompasses legal views and viewpoints, norms, institutions, as well as behavioral relations based on law. Essentially, the high level of legal culture in the *Rechtsstaat* signifies a culture of recognition, protection, and realization of human rights and freedoms as among the highest values of society.[8] Without this full-fledged recognition, it is simply not feasible to achieve an advanced level of legal awareness and an established legal culture. The value component, or axiological component, is of relevance here. Fundamental rights and freedoms can be said

---

[3] David E. Guinn, "Human Rights as Peacemaker: An Integrative Theory of International Human Rights", *Human Rights Quarterly*, Vol. 38, No. 3 (August 2016), pp. 754–786, at 755.

[4] The following definition of Rechtsstaat based on an earlier offered description of the concept by Leonov was proposed by this author: "State of Law represents a form of organization of political power characterized by rule of law, legitimacy of power, and a high prestige and efficiency of the law, that ensure legal protection of the individuals and their unimpeded use of their democratic rights and freedoms in their legitimate (lawful) interests." See Rustam Atadjanov, "Building the State of Law (Rechtsstaat) in the Countries of Central Asia: an Unachievable Dream or Realistic Objective?" Law and State 3(92) (2021): 53, at 57.

[5] Rustam Atadjanov, "Building the State of Law (Rechtsstaat) in the Countries of Central Asia: an Unachievable Dream or Realistic Objective?" Law and State 3(92) (2021): 53, at 59.

[6] Ibid.

[7] Ibid.

[8] Ibid., at 60.

to be a societal value of legal nature, and hence there is another—value-oriented—connection between human rights and law. For all these reasons, human rights and freedoms, as well as their provision and realization are of the utmost importance for establishing the other components of the *Rechtsstaat*, such as the principle of rule of law and a functioning civil society.

Fourth, the concept of human rights plays a major role in international law.[9] International human rights law or IHRL actually exists, it is an objective fact. This branch of public international law has been developing quite dynamically, with a wide range of well-established treaty sources and customary rules. Along with other important legal regimes in international law, such as international humanitarian[10] and criminal law, IHRL, applicable both during peacetime and armed conflict, comprises a mutually complementary rather than a mutually exclusive set of norms and principles.

Fifth, human rights are more than just a legal category. They are in fact also predominantly a public law concept. The following brief arguments support this proposition. The violators of human rights are mostly—although not exclusively—states, with IHRL imposing the corresponding obligations and duties (to respect the rights of individuals) upon state actors.[11] It is the state that bears the primary responsibility for providing proper conditions in order to make sure that the rights and freedoms of all members of the society are duly protected and realized. Further, human rights represent a normative form of interaction between people, organization ("orderizing") of their relationships with one another, coordination of their acts and activities, prevention of contradictions as well as confrontations and conflicts.[12] In other words, human rights set out the necessary normative conditions and ways of life. Consequently, they are needed by any state that aims at ensuring its society functions normally. This state—read "public"—element is all the more apparent when we recall the imperative role of democratic concepts such as human rights in key legal ideas such as the *Rechtsstaat* and rule of law.[13]

When it comes to the connection between the public law dimension of human rights and HRE, there are practical reasons why the dissemination of knowledge on human rights, starting with formal education in this sphere, should highlight the

---

[9] Anthony D'Amato, "The Concept of Human Rights in International Law", *Columbia Law Review*, Oct., 1982, Vol. 82, No. 6 (Oct., 1982), pp. 1110–1159, at 1111.

[10] International Committee of the Red Cross, "IHL and Human Rights", 29 October 2010, available at https://www.icrc.org/en/document/ihl-human-rights-law (last accessed 4 September 2022).

[11] See cf John H. Knox, "Horizontal Human Rights Law", *The American Journal of International Law*, Jan., 2008, Vol. 102, No. 1 (Jan., 2008), pp. 1–47. It is difficult to argue that private actors such as individuals, corporations and other non-state actors (e.g., armed groups) cannot breach human rights.

[12] Vadik Nersesyants (ed.), "Problems of the Common Theory of Law and State", 2nd ed. (Moscow, Norma, INFRA-M, 2020), at 242.

[13] The rule of law has been defined elsewhere as follows: "A principle of governance in which all persons, institutions and entities, public and private, including the State itself, are accountable to laws that are publicly promulgated, equally enforced and independently adjudicated, and which are consistent with international human rights norms and standards." Rustam Atadjanov, "Building the State of Law (Rechtsstaat) in the Countries of Central Asia: an Unachievable Dream or Realistic Objective?" *Law and State* 3(92) (2021): 53, at 59.

(public) law aspects. This is needed in order to make it clear to those being educated that the duty to establish the necessary legal protection frameworks for human rights lie first and foremost with the state. This does not in any way refute the famous proposition by Francis Lieber regarding the rights and duties paradigm: "no right without its duty, no duty without its right"; in fact, it only reinforces it. Both states and individuals have certain duties in terms of reciprocating rights. However, states have an especially important duty, not least due to the enormous potential, control, and resources they have at their disposal compared to individuals. Learning about how rights and duties work will contribute to the development of an advanced legal culture in any given society. This is especially true in regions such as Central Asia where so much still remains to be done in terms of raising legal awareness, including in the sphere of human rights and fundamental freedoms. For this reason alone (and there are certainly others), proper systematic dissemination of human rights knowledge is crucial. This may, as it does in Central Asia, encounter some of the problems discussed in some detail below (see Sect. 4). What follows is a short description of the current situation regarding teaching human rights/human rights law in Central Asian contexts.

3 Human Rights in the Education Sector in Central Asian States

Human rights education should not be regarded as an optional extra to a law curriculum in the formal education sector in the countries of Central Asia. Like many other countries, Central Asian states are obliged under IHRL to provide education aimed at strengthening respect for human rights.[14] The overview in the following sub-chapters does not purport to be exhaustive or comprehensive but highlights and briefly comments on the main elements of the formal education systems at university level (except for Turkmenistan for which there is no reliable and publicly accessible information).

---

[14] Amnesty International, "Mapping the State of Human Rights Education in Formal Secondary Education in Kyrgyzstan", April 2021, available at: www.amnesty.org/en/wp-content/uploads/2021/05/EUR5841202021ENGLISH.pdf (last accessed 4 September 2022), at 4. Hereinafter: Amnesty Report.

3.1 Kazakhstan

Kazakhstan has a highly centralized top-down political system that leaves little political, administrative, and fiscal authority to the lower levels of a clearly defined hierarchy.[15] This is also reflected in the education system, which is characterized by extensive planning and norms. Kazakhstan uses national strategic planning to broadly set out a vision for the country, but also to regulate every aspect of the education system at the central level.[16] Education in Kazakhstan is divided into pre-primary education, school education (including primary, lower secondary, and upper general or vocational secondary education), post-secondary, and tertiary education.[17]

A number of higher education institutions, both public and private, have the following courses in their bachelor's programs and course catalogues: "Human Rights Advocacy/International Human Rights Law" (KAZGUU), "Human Rights Protection" (Al-Farabi Kazakh National University), "International Human Rights Law" (KIMEP University), "Human Rights: Theory and Practice of Realization," and "International System of Human Rights Protection" (Karaganda Buketov University).[18] These specialized courses are offered alongside profile subjects such as "Public International Law," "International Public Law," and courses based on other specific branches of international law (e.g., "International Criminal Law," "International Humanitarian Law," "International Criminal Procedure," "Law of International Organizations," "Diplomatic and Consular Law," etc.).[19] Higher education subsequently proceeds to some advanced human rights-related courses for lawyers at master's level. Part of these courses is taught by holders of foreign degrees (i.e., professors with terminal degrees from universities in Western and Eastern Europe). Accordingly, it can be concluded that there is a relatively strong human rights component in the educational programs of the major universities in Kazakhstan.[20]

---

[15] OECD / The World Bank (2015), OECD Reviews of School Resources: Kazakhstan 2015, OECD Publishing, Paris, at 29. Available at: http://dx.doi.org/10.1787/9789264245891-en (last accessed 4 September 2022).

[16] Ibid.

[17] OECD / The World Bank (2015), OECD Reviews of School Resources: Kazakhstan 2015, OECD Publishing, Paris, at 37. Available at: http://dx.doi.org/10.1787/9789264245891-en (last accessed 4 September 2022).

[18] This list is only exemplary and non-exhaustive; within the chapter's volume constraints it would be unrealistic to list all existing courses for all public and private universities.

[19] The latest and more detailed updated information on these universities and their curricula may be found at the following links: https://kls.kazguu.kz/ru/katalog/, https://www.kaznu.kz/en/24665/page/, https://www.kimep.kz/school-of-law/en/llb-program/, https://buketov.edu.kz/en/page/bakalavr (last accessed 4 September 2022).

[20] As for the existence of human rights law textbooks and teaching aids in Kazakhstan, the instructors especially those from foreign countries tend to employ for their respective IHRL classes the available works and books on human rights law written in English. There is practically no local textbook on the matter in Russian.

3.2 Kyrgyzstan

According to the available reports, there is currently no comprehensive system of human rights education that is part of Kyrgyzstan's formal education system.[21] As maintained by Amnesty International, such a system would include (but would not be restricted to) a national human rights curriculum, programs and teaching packages for teaching human rights in line with international mechanisms, and professional training and development courses for teachers (or a system of regular monitoring and evaluation of teaching quality).[22]

Some universities teach human rights-related disciplines as part of their curricula, primarily within their undergraduate programs. One example is "International Human Rights Law" and "Business and Human Rights" at the American University of Central Asia in Bishkek.[23] Another example is "International Human Rights Law" at Ala-Too International University in Bishkek.[24] However, the majority of universities have not introduced the key elements of human rights into their curriculum (public universities, in particular), at least based on the available and accessible sources of information. This status quo suggests the somewhat surprising conclusion that in Kyrgyzstan, once dubbed an "island of democracy" in the region, the teaching of (international) human rights law and standards has not been deeply integrated into or systematically applied across all institutions of higher education.

3.3 Tajikistan

Unfortunately, practically no reliable information regarding the undergraduate study curricula of public universities in Tajikistan is publicly accessible. Unlike its neighbors Kyrgyzstan and Kazakhstan, Tajikistan does not make this information public, with one exception: the Russian-Tajik Slavonic University, which regularly teaches a course entitled "Safeguarding and Protection of Civil Rights" at its Faculty of Law.[25] The fact that since 2006, the Law Faculty of the Tajik National University has had a specialized Chair (Department) of Human Rights and Comparative Law suggests that they are specific courses on human rights for undergraduates.[26] The programs

---

[21] Amnesty Report, *supra* note 15, at 7.

[22] Ibid.

[23] Available at https://auca.kg/en/law_current_undergrad_courses/ (last accessed 4 September 2022).

[24] Available at http://alatoo.edu.kg/view/public/pages/page.xhtml?id=13663#gsc.tab=0 (last accessed 4 September 2022).

[25] This information may be found in Russian at ww.rtsu.tj/ru/faculties/yuridicheskiy-fakultet/Расписания%20весенний%200063;еместр-юридичесСАий%20факультет%202021-2022%20у.г.PDF (last accessed 4 September 2022).

[26] No curriculum listing is currently available online to confirm such a suggestion.

and curricula of other higher education institutions in the country cannot be verified due to the lack of accessible online sources.

3.4 Uzbekistan

In Uzbekistan, a number of programs and initiatives on human rights education have recently been announced. In 2019, the parliament (*Oliy Majlis*) adopted a National Program of Action for the Implementation of the Provisions of the UN Declaration on Human Rights Education and Training.[27] In 2020, a Presidential Decree on the National Strategy on Human Rights was adopted. The Decree contained provisions on increasing legal literacy in the sphere of human rights which included, *inter alia*, the development of proposals for the introduction of training courses (textbooks) "Human Rights," "Women's Rights," and "Children's Rights" in state higher education institutions and general education institutions.[28] Subsequently, in 2021 a special National Commission for Human Rights Education was established and one of its specific tasks is to develop a National Program for Human Rights Education.[29] Although these are all undeniably positive developments, confirming and finding up-to-date information on follow-up to any of these initiatives is a challenge, as such information is not made fully or promptly accessible.

According to the available study programs and curriculum lists of leading universities, there are some undergraduate courses on human rights. This is the case for the Faculty of Public Law at Tashkent State University of Law, for example, where a course called "Human Rights" is offered (for 2nd year students),[30] and as part of the bachelor's degree program under the "Jurisprudence" specialization of the University of World Economy and Diplomacy, a course entitled "Human Rights" is offered for 2nd, 3rd, and 4th years.[31] Undergraduate students of the Faculty of Social Sciences, Department of Civil Society and Law at the National University of Uzbekistan are also offered a course somewhat curiously named "International and Human Rights."[32] In addition, one of the peripheral universities, the Karakalpak State University named after Berdakh has a functioning chair in its Faculty of Law,

---

[27] See the text of the relevant Joint Decree (without annexes) in Russian at https://lex.uz/docs/449 3780 (last accessed 4 September 2022).

[28] Full text is available in Russian at https://lex.uz/docs/4872357 (last accessed 4 September 2022).

[29] The relevant news in this regard may be found at https://bigasia.ru/content/news/society/spetsialn aya-komissiya-zaymyetsya-razvitiem-obrazovaniya-v-oblasti-prav-cheloveka-v-uzbekistane/ (last accessed 4 September 2022).

[30] Information available at https://tsul.uz/uz/general-page/Faculty%20of%20Law-QS (last accessed 4 September 2022).

[31] See at https://www.uwed.uz/en/pages/educational-plans (last accessed 4 September 2022).

[32] See at https://nuu.uz/en/fuqarolik-jamiyati-va-huquq-kafedrasi/ (last accessed 4 September 2022).

again with the curious title of "Chair of Human Rights, State Law and Administration."[33] Unfortunately, no information is available as to what exact courses the faculty teaches.

However, human rights subjects are mostly taught in a generalist way rather than as a category of public or international law—this is illustrated by the respective course titles and the curriculum structure. There appears to be no unified, coherent approach to teaching IHRL as a legal discipline. Further, in some universities, such courses are only offered for students in certain years, while other universities offer human rights courses at almost all levels, except for freshman. These inconsistencies could be remedied if, in parallel to national ad hoc plans, domestic education standards in each of the Central Asian contexts, studies were to consistently stipulate human rights law courses.

4 Challenges to Effective Instruction on Human Rights

Some of the difficulties encountered by instructors in human rights and IHRL disciplines in the Central Asian region are similar in nature to the typical challenges to teaching public international law. Others are strongly associated with factors specific to the region. Correspondingly, this section is divided into two short parts: the first deals with the challenges resulting from the inherent connection between human rights law and public international law (understandably, this category of challenges would surely not be endemic to this region only); the second encompasses those challenges that are directly related to particularities of the local context in terms of the history of the region, its politics, economics, social factors, people's mentality, religion, and culture.

The first group includes the following observations. There are university students who question the very essence of international law, and by extension IHRL, as a true legal branch or its international nature, while others doubt whether international law is still capable of solving the complicated problems of today. There are those who admit the importance of public international law from a doctrinal and theoretical perspective, but deny its practical role compared to domestic law. Further, students tend to rely on domestic legal concepts, principles, and analogies to understand international legal sources and concepts. In other words, there is a clear tendency to apply the logic of the "law of subordination" typical of domestic legal systems to the "law of coordination" which characterizes international law and IHRL. The influence of political considerations on the application and implementation of international law must be noted, too. As is well known, the role of the existence or absence of political will of governments when it comes to domestic implementation and dissemination of knowledge on treaty and customary IHRL is crucial. This often leads to a misperception among students of international law and IHRL that the entire international law structure represents a regulatory system governed by Realpolitik

---

[33] See in Russian at https://karsu.uz/ru/ (last accessed 4 September 2022).

rather than cosmopolitan axiology and legal values. All these difficulties ultimately contribute to students' skeptical attitudes toward modern international law.

When it comes to the second group of challenges, one problem lies in governments' and populations' general perception of law and its dissemination. According to this author elsewhere:

> Law is oftentimes regarded by certain authorities [in Central Asia] as merely an instrument, i.e., a functional tool to support exclusively the state system and national interests but not as a value on its own or a means to help improve the well-being of the society. This, along with a traditional conformist mentality and general distrust of the people toward legal rules as serving only the interests of the State, results in attitudes such as legal nihilism and low legal culture. Adding to this is an underestimation of the influence and power of the respective progressive academic schools of legal thought which are not sufficiently represented by prominent academics and lack proper tools, textbooks, individual and collective monographs, reference editions, etc. While the constitutional systems of all post-Soviet States include elements of the democratic, liberal, secular and social State, and encompass most of the categories of fundamental constitutional/human rights (civil, political, economic, social and cultural) in their respective Supreme Laws, their implementation in practice remains another major challenge. This in large part may be attributed to the preponderance of statist and positivist approaches to the law in almost all countries of the region.[34]

All the challenges mentioned in the above quote, i.e., (1) legal nihilism and low legal culture, (2) underestimation of the power of the academic schools of legal thought, and (3) statist and positivist approaches to law, equally apply to public international law, IHRL, and the academic instruction thereof. International law—and IHRL by extension—is part of law as such. Alongside the general attitudes toward law, international law is also often perceived by both students and teachers as merely an instrument of power politics and government decision-making rather than an important value-oriented legal phenomenon and essential tool to ensure peace, security, and the well-being of the people, including their individual rights. This affects the teaching of human rights law courses to undergraduate students: in my opinion, before embarking on learning the tenets of IHRL, students need first to have a solid basic understanding of law and legal theory, so as to be able to appreciate the role of the different branches of law but also to be able to critically reflect on legal norms and principles operating at the international level and protecting individual and collective rights.

Furthermore, a well-known problem with the idea of human rights and international law lies in it being viewed essentially as a product of Western culture, promoting predominantly Western values and interests that are often considered alien or even incompatible with Eastern/non-Western culture(s). A sub-concept of this "Westernism," so-called Eurocentrism, that is a European bias, may serve as an illustrative example in this regard. This phenomenon has long been noted and commented upon by scholars.[35] Being part of Asia, Central Asia is also prone to such attitudes. This often necessitates reconstructing or restructuring the older curricula

---

[34] Rustam Atadjanov, "Building the State of Law (Rechtsstaat) in the Countries of Central Asia: an Unachievable Dream or Realistic Objective?" *Law and State* 3(92) (2021): 53, at 64.

[35] See for an instructive overview and useful discussion: B. S. Chimni, "Is There an Asian Approach to International Law? Questions, Theses and Reflections" in *Asian Yearbook of International Law*,

to encompass non-Western scholarship of international law and human rights but also means dealing with students' cultural relativistic points of view.

Finally, the scarcity of library resources on IHRL at the higher education establishments in the Central Asian region needs to be noted. The majority of the modern literature on human rights law—is difficult to obtain in these libraries, at least in paper format. This might partially be related to the very limited funding for library stocks, but it may also well be due to a lack of interest and insufficient motivation to order foreign titles written in English to be made available for students being educated in universities where the language of instruction is English. Coupled with the lack of teaching aids and textbooks on the subject in Russian or in English, this problem represents a major issue to be tackled at the systemic level. In the author's opinion, a lack of scholarly resources does not bode well for effective instruction in any discipline.

5 Ways Ahead for Human Rights Education in Central Asia

In order to address the challenges of HRE in Central Asia described above, I propose the following potentially useful approaches. First, I suggest that, to make human rights instruction much more systematic and holistic, all interested parties, beginning with the relevant state entities, allocate and expand the necessary resources.[36] Commitment to human rights could better be demonstrated in practice, including by way of providing the necessary financial means to improve the relevant education systems.

Second, with a view to addressing the key issue of legal nihilism and the low level of legal culture, proper, comprehensive, theoretical, doctrinal, and practical dissemination of knowledge and coverage of legal principles in a systematic manner appears necessary. It is proposed that these countries further develop and expand their respective schools of legal thought, which could contribute to strengthening the role of the law and its efficiency, not only in the state's interests but, first and foremost, for the benefit of society.[37] Moreover, taking into account attitudes of local populations and mentality of the people, the dissemination of legal values and ideas needs to be integrated into the education system at an early stage. This is not only a question

---

B. S. Chimni, Miyoshi Masahiro and Thio Li-Ann, eds. (Brill, 2011), 264; Jean d'Aspremont, "International Law in Asia: the Limits to the Western Constitutionalist and Liberal Doctrines", in *Asian Yearbook of International Law*, B. S. Chimni, Miyoshi Masahiro and Thio Li-Ann, eds. (Brill, 2009), *passim*.

[36] Amnesty International, "Human Rights Education. High Level Overview of HRE Instruments, Mechanisms to be Considered in Central Asia", EUR 04/9074/2018, 11 September 2018, at 5.

[37] Rustam Atadjanov, "Building the State of Law (Rechtsstaat) in the Countries of Central Asia: an Unachievable Dream or Realistic Objective?" *Law and State* 3(92) (2021): 53, at 65. See also Amnesty International, "Human Rights Education. High Level Overview of HRE Instruments, Mechanisms to be Considered in Central Asia", EUR 04/9074/2018, 11 September 2018, at 5.

of developing schools of legal thought. If the understanding of law as a basic value, and not just a tool, along with an effective explanation of the idea of human rights, true constitutionalism, and civil society, are not covered during the early stages of education (high school), gaps in legal awareness and legal culture will arise.[38]

Third, and building on the previous recommendation, it appears important for human rights instructors, educators, and teachers in Central Asia to apply the so-called value-based approach to their teaching. This approach suggests a contextualized explanation of IHRL from the perspective of its contribution to the protection of fundamental values of humankind, such as respect for human rights and fundamental freedoms, but also global peace and security. It is in line with a more general view on the law as being a "protective" set of rules rather than simply a "regulative" system. International law and IHRL's fundamental premise that they serve the needs of the global/international community and individuals by way of maintaining, securing the achievement of, and protecting the key values of humanity ("humanity" as in "humankind") is more likely to be clearly understood when the aforementioned approach is applied.

Fourth, and finally, special attention has to be paid to the quality of the instructors who deliver the human rights courses. Human rights law and IHRL must be taught by properly trained teachers and professors, otherwise human rights education reforms will not be viable. If teachers and trainers are not able to explain, e.g., the difference between a right-holder and a duty-bearer, cannot themselves identify human rights violations or abuses or give relevant examples, or properly analyze case studies, the adoption and improvement of human rights curricula/programs may in fact negatively influence the respect for human rights in the countries of Central Asia. Training of educators would need to be approached consistently, for example by supporting their participation in various types of human rights events, providing relevant on-the-job training, inviting international experts to speak, and recruiting instructors who have graduated from foreign universities with a focus on public international law and human rights.[39]

6 Conclusion

The discussion in this chapter covered several challenges and problematic issues that education systems in Central Asia experience in terms of teaching human rights-related disciplines in high schools and universities. It grouped these challenges into two main categories: those pertaining to the unique nature of IHRL itself as being part of public international law, and those related to and flowing from local contexts in the region. By subsequently proposing certain potentially useful recommendations and approaches (such as, for example, value-based approaches), this chapter offers

---

[38] Amnesty International, "Human Rights Education. High Level Overview of HRE Instruments, Mechanisms to be Considered in Central Asia", EUR 04/9074/2018, 11 September 2018, at 5–6.
[39] Ibid.

not only a description of the problems human rights instructors encounter in their work but also provides a range of potentially useful methods or tools to address those problems.

This chapter in no way purports to provide a comprehensive description or range of methods and tools. Instead, its suggestions should be taken as a minimal starting point for improving the teaching of human rights in the region where the latter's role is oftentimes ignored or insufficiently recognized. While some instructors (including the author of this work) have already begun to employ several of these methods and approaches, for others this might not yet be the case. With this in mind, the author hopes that this piece will serve as an instrumental tool for instructors and educators who genuinely want to improve their teaching of human rights law.

In order for IHRL to be applied effectively and successfully in Central Asia, it must first be learnt and understood properly by government representatives and populations alike. For this, we rely on high school and university teachers and instructors to carry out their duties professionally. In the modern world, where IHRL, with its value system, is constantly challenged and its norms and principles are often blatantly violated, the task of these instructors becomes all the more crucial. Certainly, all the challenges described above need to be addressed in a principled, systematic, and contextualized manner. Considering that the education systems in the region, along with the state and legal systems, are still developing and continue to face many hurdles, this will not be easy. One needs to be patient but also determined. That said, when was anything about human rights law and its proper realization ever easy? And the very same applies to effective teaching of human rights law as well.

References

Amnesty International (2018) Human rights education. High level overview of HRE instruments, mechanisms to be considered in Central Asia, EUR 04/9074/2018
Amnesty International (2021) Mapping the state of human rights education in formal secondary education in Kyrgyzstan
Atadjanov R (2021) Building the state of law (Rechtsstaat) in the countries of Central Asia: an unachievable dream or realistic objective? Law State 3(92):53
Chimni B (2011) Is there an Asian approach to international law? Questions, theses and reflections. In: Chimni B et al (ed) Asian yearbook of international law. Brill, Nijhoff, vol 14, pp 249–264
D'Amato A (1982) The concept of human rights in international law. Columbia Law Rev 82(6):1,110–1,159
D'Aspremont J (2009) International law in Asia: the limits to the Western constitutionalist and liberal doctrines. In: Chimni B et al (ed) Asian yearbook of international law. Brill, Nijhoff, vol 13, pp 27–49
Guinn D (2016) Human rights as peacemaker: an integrative theory of international human rights. Hum Rights Q 38(3):754–786
Knox J (2008) Horizontal human rights law. Am J Int Law 102(1):1–47
Nersesyants V (2020) Problems of the common theory of law and state, 2nd ed. Norma, INFRA-M, Moscow
OECD/World Bank (2015) OECD reviews of school resources: Kazakhstan 2015. OECD Publishing, Paris

Open Access This chapter is licensed under the terms of the Creative Commons Attribution 4.0 International License (http://creativecommons.org/licenses/by/4.0/), which permits use, sharing, adaptation, distribution and reproduction in any medium or format, as long as you give appropriate credit to the original author(s) and the source, provide a link to the Creative Commons license and indicate if changes were made.

The images or other third party material in this chapter are included in the chapter's Creative Commons license, unless indicated otherwise in a credit line to the material. If material is not included in the chapter's Creative Commons license and your intended use is not permitted by statutory regulation or exceeds the permitted use, you will need to obtain permission directly from the copyright holder.

Transnational Higher Education—The Case of Kazakhstan

Eriks Varpahovskis and Anna Kuteleva

1 Introduction

The demise of the Soviet system and ideology toppled the Soviet—de facto Russian—monopoly in higher education. The Central Asian republics of Kazakhstan, Kyrgyzstan, Tajikistan, Turkmenistan, and Uzbekistan had to remodel their national systems of higher education to adapt to new socioeconomic circumstances (Smolentseva et al. 2018). While all five states have struggled with the Soviet path dependency and enduring legacies (Azimbayeva 2017), they managed step by step to reform their higher education systems. This was not a linear process, but internationalization has become a key factor in the reform efforts and continues to be one of the major policy priorities. The five states at least partially adopted the European Bologna Process, launched and expanded academic and student mobility programs, globalized education by inviting international universities to set up their branches, and introduced new disciplines, such as marketing and business management. In Central Asia, this was a state-driven process with national leaders aiming to obtain modern technologies and improve human resources to ease the post-socialist transition (Varpahovskis and Kuteleva forthcoming).

As scholars of transnational education and soft power point out, inviting foreign institutions to establish a presence in the country can have an impact on the local culture and values (e.g., Altbach and Peterson 2015; Bertelsen 2012; Wojciuk 2018; Knight and de Wit 2018). The transformation of Central Asian education systems

---

E. Varpahovskis (✉)
Researcher, Duy Tan University in Vietnam, Da Nang, Vietnam
e-mail: erix.vars@gmail.com

A. Kuteleva
School of Social Science and Humanities, University of Wolverhampton, Wolverhampton, UK
e-mail: A.Kuteleva@wlv.ac.uk

© The Author(s) 2023
A. Mihr and C. Wittke (eds.), *Human Rights Dissemination in Central Asia*, SpringerBriefs in Political Science,
https://doi.org/10.1007/978-3-031-27972-0_5

through opening up to foreign institutions is intriguing, as in addition to technological and market-oriented specializations, these institutions have introduced value-oriented subjects and, in particular, human rights education. The scholarship exploring the role and impact of Transnational Higher Education Institutions (THEIs) on human rights education is scarce and fragmented (e.g., Steiner 2002; Ó'Cuinn and Skogly 2016; Miller-Idriss and Hanauer 2011), whereas studies focused on the Central Asian republics as receivers of international human rights education via THEIs are almost absent. This study seeks to address this gap by exploring the role of THEIs in Central Asia based on the case of Kazakhstan. The following sections discuss the conceptual and methodological framework of this study, present the key results, and highlight avenues for future research.

2 Transnational Higher Education Institutions: Global Phenomenon and Regional Practice

In the context of globalization, higher education is no longer limited to national societies but transcends borders. Despite being intuitively obvious, there are competing interpretations of the concept of "transnationality" in higher education. Transnational Higher Education Institutions (THEI) have different ownership structures, objectives, strategies, and types of students. Importantly, the legal status of THEIs varies from country to country as well, and while some states welcome THEIs and offer them a lot of freedom, others strictly monitor whether THEIs conform with national regulations and restrict curricula development in particular study fields.

In this study we adopt the definition of THEIs offered by Varpahovskis (2021), which captures the notion of "transnationality" in higher education based on its institutional and pedagogical features. As such, we classify a HEI as transnational if its ownership and/or management is designed and controlled by citizens and/or organizations from a foreign country. The pedagogical features include using a foreign language or languages as the medium of instruction, adopting foreign teaching materials and course designs, and employing a distinctive teaching philosophy. Transnational higher education institutions not only address the labor market needs of host countries and contribute to local internationalization of the education agenda, but they also promote intercultural dialogue and cross-cultural understanding.

Since independence, the five Central Asia states have made consistent efforts to modernize and reform their education systems in alignment with the broader social, economic, and political transformations. In the realm of higher education, internationalization has become one of the key priorities. Today, Central Asia hosts a total of 65 THEIs (see Table 1). Universities from Russia, Turkey, Germany, the US, the UK, and other countries have established branches in Central Asia. Not all Central Asian THEIs are linked to a parent institution abroad, however. The OSCE Academy in Kyrgyzstan and the University of Central Asia (UCA), with its branches in Kyrgyzstan and Tajikistan, are cases in point. The obvious outliers are Turkmenistan

Table 1 Total number of THEIs in Central Asia, as of 2021

Host country	Total number of THEIs in host country
Kazakhstan	14
Kyrgyzstan	19
Tajikistan	4
Turkmenistan	0
Uzbekistan	28

Source Compiled and updated by authors based on a policy brief by Varpahovskis (2021)

and Tajikistan. The two THEIs that operated in Turkmenistan—a branch of the Gubkin Russian State University of Oil and Gas (2008–2012) and the International Turkmen-Turkish University (1994–2016)—abruptly lost their education licenses and were closed down by the decree of President Gurbanguly Berdimuhamedow. Tajikistan made an exception for branches of four Russian HEIs and UCA's Khorgos Campus (opened in 2017, but at risk of losing its education license in 2022). In contrast, Kyrgyzstan has rather liberal regulations for accrediting, registering, and licensing new HEIs, including transnational ones. The governments of Kazakhstan and Uzbekistan support the growth of transnational education but tightly regulate and control its providers. For instance, Kazakhstan revoked the license of THEIs that included religious courses in their curricula (see Vilkovski 2011 on the Kazakh-Kuwaiti University) or failed to satisfy local academic quality assurance requirements (e.g., the Kazakhstani-Russian University).

3 International Human Rights Education: A Conceptual Frame

The Universal Declaration of Human Rights (UN 1948) is the first formal international instrument to describe education as a means of disseminating human rights (Paragraph 2, Article 26). Hence, as early as 1948, the principle of human rights education was a means of promoting these rights, and education became an integral part of human rights discourse. The UN Declaration on Human Rights Education and Training defines human rights education as encompassing all "educational, training, information, awareness-raising and learning activities aimed at promoting universal respect for and observance of all human rights and fundamental freedoms and thus contributing, inter alia, to the prevention of human rights violations and abuses by providing persons with knowledge, skills and understanding and developing their attitudes and behaviors, to empower them to contribute to the building and promotion of a universal culture of human rights" (UN General Assembly 2011, p. 3). Yet, a single definition of human rights education cannot reflect the diversity of ways in which people around the world understand and practice their rights and respect for the rights of others, and the importance they attach to them (Dufourt 2021). In this sense, the key to the definition of human rights education lies in its purpose because, regardless of methodology or context, it always aims at developing a culture of human rights (Dufourt 2021). The essential components of such a culture therefore inform the general objectives of human rights education. This lack of conceptual clarity opens the door to a problematic all-inclusiveness and on the one hand, it makes it possible to add educational activities and programs aimed at promoting the equal dignity of human beings to the curricula of various disciplines, ranging from political science and sociology to mining engineering and computer science.

4 THEIs in Kazakhstan: A Case Study

4.1 Methodology

Kazakhstan, with its population of more than 18 million, has 122 HEIs as of the 2021-2022 academic year (Kapital.kz 2022). Among them are 14 THEIs: six are affiliated with Russia, three with the US, two with Turkey, and the UK, Germany, and Egypt each have a single representation. The UCA campus in Tekeli, several Russian HEIs, and US-affiliated branch campuses were not included in our calculations since their status could not be confirmed for the 2021–2022 academic year. We based our selection of THEIs on the study by Varpahovskis (2021) (see Table 2).

Very few of the THEIs located in Kazakhstan have a strong humanities and social sciences orientation. Instead, most of them are either Science, technology, engineering and mathematics (STEM) only or offer mixed curricula with an explicit leaning toward STEM subjects. We examine the publicly available curricula of each THEI currently operating in Kazakhstan to determine whether they offer human rights-related courses and programs. The degree of international human rights teaching is presented in our research summary in Table 2. We marked those programs that at least mention international human rights in their curricula with "yes", even when only a fraction of a course touches upon human rights. The "Details" column in Table 2 indicates the extent to which human rights are taught as part of human rights education endeavors in the selected THEI.

4.2 Human Rights Education and Country Affiliation of THEIs

Descriptive analysis of Kazakhstan-based HEIs showed that 14 institutions represent six countries: Russia, the US, Turkey, the UK, Germany, and Egypt. This

Table 2 Profiles and summary of curriculum analysis of THEIs studied

THEI name	THEI affiliation country	Curricula orientation	Human rights education in the curriculum	Details/notes	International ranking position
Chelyabinsk State University	Russia	Mixed	Yes	Required introduction to human rights courses for students majoring in International Law and an upper-level elective course International Cooperation in Human Rights and Freedom Protection	3,190 (parent university)
Lomonosov Moscow State University	Russia	Mixed	No	–	20,511
St. Petersburg Humanitarian University of Trade Unions	Russia	Mixed	No	–	22,151
Kazakh-Russian Medical University	Russia	STEM	No	–	20,399
Synergy University	Russia	Non-STEM	No	–	9,186 (parent university)
"Voskhod" branch of the Moscow Aviation Institute	Russia	Mixed	No	–	2,050 (parent university)
Ahmet Yesevi University	Turkey	Mixed	No	–	4,928
Suleyman Demirel University	Turkey	Mixed	Yes	A required Human Rights course for undergraduate students majoring in Law and Social Sciences	5,103

(continued)

Table 2 (continued)

THEI name	THEI affiliation country	Curricula orientation	Human rights education in the curriculum	Details/notes	International ranking position
Kazakhstan Institute of Management, Economics and Strategic Research (KIMEP)	US	Humanities and social sciences	Yes	Specialized elective course, 5 ECTS credits. Bachelor of Law (LLB)	7,811
Kazakh American University	US	Mixed	Yes	An undergraduate elective course International Mechanisms for Protecting Human Rights and Freedom No specialized graduate courses Some international studies and political science courses briefly mention human rights (e.g., Introduction to International Relations)	Not listed
Kazakh American Free University	US	Humanities and social sciences	Yes	International human rights law is briefly mentioned in the description of Theory of State and Law course	19,109
Kazakh-British Technical University (KBTU)	UK	STEM mixed with business administration	No	–	6,365
Kazakh-German University	Germany	Mixed	No	–	16,148
Nur-Mubarak University of Islamic Culture	Egypt	Humanities and religion	No	–	30,161

Note For THEIs that are not listed in Webometrics' university rankings, we include the parent university's ranking results

finding indicates that Kazakhstan does not hesitate to import higher education services and knowledge as well as certain cultural features that accompany higher education from multiple supplying countries, some of which may even belong to opposing political camps (e.g., the US vs. Russia). It corresponds to the idea promoted by the former President of Kazakhstan Nursultan Nazarbayev that modern Kazakhstani development should incorporate the best achievements and knowledge from various cultures (e.g., Western, Russian, Turkic, Islamic) (Varpahovskis and Kuteleva forthcoming).

While THEIs in Kazakhstan do not offer specialized degrees in international human rights law, the range of human rights education varies from a brief mention as a topic of one of the lectures to a full-scale course. Alternatively topics on human rights are incorporated and included in courses offered at the Kazakh American Free University (e.g., as a component of the course on Issues of Theory of State and Law) and Suleyman Demirel University (e.g., as a component of the International Relations undergraduate program).

The intuitive assumption that THEIs affiliated with countries designated as the "West" (e.g., the US, the UK, and Germany) provide a greater variety of human rights training than their "non-Western" counterparts is only partially correct. Some of "Western" THEIs (e.g., KBTU) have a narrow focus on STEM and do not offer any human rights courses as part of their curricula. Among "Western" HEIs, only THEIs affiliated with the US include human rights education in the form of special topic courses. Curiously, branches of HEIs affiliated with states classified as authoritarian in the Democracy Index (Economist Intelligence Unit Limited 2021) do provide general human rights courses. As such, students majoring in Criminal Law at the Chelyabinsk State University are required to take a course on International Cooperation in Humans Rights and Freedom Protection. Even the most basic analysis of the syllabus reveals that "Western" and "non-Western" THEIs opt for contrasting approaches to human rights education[1] and reporting violations.[2] Thus, international human rights education is not monopolized by THEIs representing democratic regimes.

Even though international university rankings are quite subjective (Stack 2021), the rather low international ranking of the majority of THEIs raises questions about the quality of education they offer (see Table 2). Some THEIs rank high by subject (e.g., Ahmet Yesevi University was ranked 201st of 250 in modern languages by the QS World University Rankings in 2022 (QS 2022)). However, these are not subjects that include human rights education.

Transnational higher education institutions in Kazakhstan currently do not offer courses or programs that examine how international human rights norms and standards are localized at national and regional levels. Similarly, THEIs do not offer specialized courses that examine the particularities of human rights implementation

---

[1] Course specification for Jurisprudence, criminal law specialization, 27 August 2020, Chelyabinsk State University, available at: https://csukz.ru/sveden/files/B1.V.1.09_RPD(8).pdf, p. 3.

[2] LAW4504 International Human Rights Law, 2019-2020, KIMEP, available at: https://www2.kimep.kz/anon/StAffairs/SyllabusPDF?code=LAW4504.

with a focus on gender equality and the rights of ethnic, religious, or linguistic minorities. Human rights are not taught outside programs on law and international relations. This means that human rights education in THEIs emphasizes the legal dimensions of human rights, ignoring learning by skills and learning by service approaches. Simply put, only potential lawyers and those aspiring for careers in international communications are taught about human rights.

The inclusion of general human rights courses in highly formalized curricula on law and international relations contributes to the spread of the approach that André Keet (2007, 2017) and other critical scholars of human rights (Dufourt 2021) describe as "declarationist". These courses explore human rights through the prism of universal norms and standards and the role of international institutions in promoting them. Such framing of human rights education is less likely to create opportunities for adapting course content to the social and cultural realities of the lives of the local students and are eventually likely to contribute to marginalizing students' experiences and their understanding of the world. In other words, students have limited opportunities to make meaningful connections between the context in which they are living and human rights, not as an international theory but as a potential reality for them. Moreover, although Kazakhstan strongly prefers institutions oriented toward STEM when importing THEIs (Varpahovskis and Kuteleva forthcoming), the focus on developing human rights culture implies that there is a place for human rights education even in STEM curricula. For example, human rights education is relevant for mining engineering students, since resource exploration activities often interfere with the lives of local populations.

Importantly, syllabuses of basic political science courses—an introduction to politics or political institutions—do not explicitly include human rights topics. As a result, citizenship and human rights are separated in the curricula, almost torn apart as if the rights of citizens were not based on human rights. This effectively ignores Article 21 of the Universal Declaration of Human Rights, which establishes citizenship as a civil and political right of every human being: "Everyone has the right to take part in the government of his country, directly or through freely chosen representatives".

Overall, the number of disciplines that include human rights courses is limited (e.g., to an elective course or a few lectures in the International Relations or International Law syllabuses), which indicates that human rights education is overlooked and marginalized in the curricula of THEIs. Importantly, human rights education offered by THEIs in Kazakhstan is not rooted in the local contexts and thus cannot pursue its primary pedagogical objective, namely emancipating students and developing their power to act.

5 Human Rights Education in THEIs: Opportunities and Challenges

As the analysis of Kazakhstan's THEI policy (Varpahovskis and Kuteleva forthcoming) demonstrates, the Kazakh state perceives THEIs as media of knowledge and skills transfer that have the potential to advance national economic development. The state promotes transnational STEM training for various industrial sectors, as well as business administration and soft skills training (e.g., marketing) that would help Kazakhstan to integrate into the global market. To put it mildly, human rights education is not a priority for the state.

Human rights education has never been a part of the brand of Russia's or Turkey's universities, with both countries struggling domestically with promoting human rights literacy and developing respect for human rights among the citizens (Çayır and Bağlı 2011, Gerber 2017, Sen and Starkey 2017). Western THEIs in Kazakhstan seem to prioritize the steady streams of revenue, ignoring the local human rights challenges. Given that the public discussion of HEIs operating overseas is limited (if it exists at all), the significance of their human rights obligations is often overlooked. As Gearóid Ó Cuinn (2016) accurately puts it, "often there appears to be a misplaced faith that the campus gate insulates a branch campus from the ills of a local setting".[3] In sum, there are no stakeholders—internal or external—interested in turning THEIs into providers of human rights education in Kazakhstan.

Besides expanding the scope of research to include other Central Asian countries when investigating the presence of human rights education in the curricula of THEIs, scholars might attempt to test the assumption that international human rights education is a specific feature of US-affiliated THEIs in Central Asia. As of 2021, there are four US-affiliated THEIs operating in the region: three in Kyrgyzstan and one in Uzbekistan (Varpahovskis 2021). Moreover, Arizona University has recently announced plans to open a branch in Kazakhstan (Bulatkulova 2022). Further, a comparative study of approaches to human rights education of THEIs affiliated with the US and Western European states would provide a more nuanced and balanced understanding of this field in Central Asia. Likewise, it is worth looking into the content of human rights education more rigorously to explore differences in interpretation and teaching models in THEIs representing "Western" and "non-Western" institutions.

Finally, even though human rights education is definitely an important subject of research and teaching, scholars and higher education experts should question whether the regional job market requires specialists in this field. Availability of professional opportunities may determine the progress of human rights education in the Central Asian region. Thus careful investigation into the links between human rights education and opportunities to act and change through human rights empowerment and implementation is needed. Otherwise, extensive teaching of international human

---

[3] For a more detailed discussion, see Ó Cuinn, G and Skogly, S (2016). Understanding human rights obligations of states engaged in public activity overseas: the case of transnational education. The International Journal of Human Rights 20(6): 761–784.

rights-related subjects that do not address demand on the domestic job market could be seen as interference in internal affairs and an attempt at indoctrination. Further, scholars and educators should inquire about awareness of and interest in human rights among prospective students. These factors may also influence THEIs' intention to offer students human rights education (Wittke and Rabinovych 2022; Wittke 2022).

References

Altbach P, Peterson P (2015) Higher education as a projection of America's soft power. Soft power superpowers. Routledge, London and New York, pp 69–85

Azimbayeva G (2017) Comparing post-Soviet changes in higher education governance in Kazakhstan, Russia, and Uzbekistan. Cogent Educ 4(1):1399968. https://doi.org/10.1080/2331186X.2017.1399968

Bertelsen R (2012) Private foreign-affiliated universities, the state, and soft power: the American University of Beirut and the American University in Cairo. Foreign Policy Anal 8(3):293–311

Bulatkulova S (2022) University of Arizona Campus in Kazakhstan Prepares To Welcome First Students In September. Astana Times. https://astanatimes.com/2022/04/university-of-arizona-campus-in-kazakhstan-prepares-to-welcome-first-students-in-september/#:~:text=Earlier%20in%202021%2C%20the%20Kazakh,the%20University%20of%20Arizona's%20model.

Çayır K, Bağlı M (2011) 'No-one respects them anyway': secondary school students' perceptions of human rights education in Turkey. Intercult Educ 22(1):1–14

Dufourt P (2021) Promouvoir un enseignement pluraliste des droits humains. Quelles conditions épistémologiques? Cahiers Jean Moulin (7). https://journals.openedition.org/cjm/1322

Economist Intelligence Unit Limited (2021) Democracy Index 2021: the China challenge. https://www.eiu.com/n/campaigns/democracy-index-2021/

Gerber T (2017) Public opinion on human rights in Putin-era Russia: continuities, changes, and sources of variation. J Hum Rights 16(3):314–331

Kapital.kz (2022) V akademicheskiy reyting universitetov popal vsego odin kazakhstanskiy vuz [Only one Kazakh university is included in the academic ranking of universities]. https://kapital.kz/gosudarstvo/105734/v-akademicheskiy-reyting-universitetov-popal-vsego-odin-kazakhstanskiy-vuz.html

Keet A (2007) Human rights education or human rights in education: a conceptual analysis. Doctoral dissertation, University of Pretoria

Keet A (2017) Does human rights education exist? Int J Hum Rights Educ 1(1):6

Knight J, De Wit H (2018) Internationalization of higher education: past and future. Int Higher Educ 95:2–4

Miller-Idriss C, Hanauer E (2011) Transnational higher education: offshore campuses in the Middle East. Comp Educ 47(2):181–207

Ó Cuinn G (2016) Transnational education and human rights obligations. University World News: The Global Window on Higher education. https://www.universityworldnews.com/post.php?story=20160329133947564

Ó Cuinn G, Skogly S (2016) Understanding human rights obligations of states engaged in public activity overseas: the case of transnational education. Int J Hum Rights 20(6):761–784

QS (2022) Khoja Akhmet Yassawi International Kazakh-Turkish University. QS WUR Ranking by Subject: Modern Languages. https://www.topuniversities.com/universities/khoja-akhmet-yassawi-international-kazakh-turkish-university

Sen A, Starkey H (2017) The rise and fall of citizenship and human rights education in Turkey. JSSE-J Soc Sci Educ 85–97

Smolentseva A, Huisman J, Froumin I (2018) Transformation of Higher Education Institutional Landscape in Post-Soviet Countries: From Soviet Model to Where? In: 25 years of transformations of higher education Systems in Post-Soviet Countries. Palgrave Macmillan, Cham, pp 1–43

Stack M (ed) (2021) Global university rankings and the politics of knowledge. University of Toronto Press

Steiner H (2002) The university's critical role in the human rights movement. Harvard Hum Rights J 15:317

UN (1948) Universal Declaration of Human Rights. https://www.un.org/en/about-us/universal-declaration-of-human-rights

UN General Assembly (2011) United Nations Declaration on Human Rights Education

Varpahovskis E, Kuteleva A (forthcoming) Does soft power make authoritarian regimes import universities? Framing analysis of discourses around transnational higher education institutions in Kazakhstan. In: Chitty N, Ji L, Rawnsley G (eds) Routledge handbook of soft power, 2nd edn. Routledge, London, New York

Varpahovskis E (2021) Patterns and State Strategies of Transnational Higher Education Institutions in Central Asia. Policy Brief #75. OSCE Academy, Bishkek

Vilkovski D (2011) Arabo-Musul'manskiye Organizatsii v Kazakhstane: Vneshneye Vozdeystviye na Islamskoye Obnovleniye [Arab-Muslim Organizations in Kazakhstan: External Impact on Islamic Renaissance]. Rossia i Musulmanskiy Mir 11:57–73

Wittke C, Rabinovych M (2022) Troubled nexuses between international and domestic law in the post- soviet space, Review of Central and East European Law 47(3–4):249–267. https://doi.org/10.1163/15730352-47030001 (Open Access)

Wittke C (ed.) (2022) Post-soviet conflict potentials. Abingdon-on-Thames. https://www.routledge.com/9781032304007, New York: Routledge, Taylor & Francis Ltd

Wojciuk A (2018) Higher education as a soft power in international relations. In: Handbook of cultural security. Edward Elgar Publishing, Cheltenham and Northampton

Open Access This chapter is licensed under the terms of the Creative Commons Attribution 4.0 International License (http://creativecommons.org/licenses/by/4.0/), which permits use, sharing, adaptation, distribution and reproduction in any medium or format, as long as you give appropriate credit to the original author(s) and the source, provide a link to the Creative Commons license and indicate if changes were made.

The images or other third party material in this chapter are included in the chapter's Creative Commons license, unless indicated otherwise in a credit line to the material. If material is not included in the chapter's Creative Commons license and your intended use is not permitted by statutory regulation or exceeds the permitted use, you will need to obtain permission directly from the copyright holder.

Redesigning the Law Curriculum in Uzbekistan

Aziz Ismatov and Manuchehr Kudratov

1 Introduction

Since 1991, Uzbekistan has been carrying out reforms in the higher education (hereinafter, HE) sector in a rigorous and top-down manner. The HE-related laws that were adopted contained positive intentions, including upgrading the general legal framework for HE and improving the quality of degrees by offering new courses. After 30 years of postsocialist transition in Uzbekistan, and despite initially far-reaching goals, practical experience has shown that laws on HE addressed vital matters in largely abstract terms. While laws on HE, for instance, paved the way for establishing several universities that offered legal education, they did not grant adequate autonomy to these institutions in such essential matters as curriculum and syllabus design, teaching and assessment, graduation requirements, and financial issues. The result of this process is that today, legal education is characterized by a centralized structure and traditional state-centered approach with the government departments at the top (such as the Ministry of Justice or the Ministry of Specialized Higher and Secondary Education) and law faculties at the very bottom. The problem with this structure is that it reflects a former socialist doctrine of placing the state rather than the individual at the center of legal relations, as per the contemporary constitutional goal.[1]

---

[1] For a more in-depth discussion on this, see: A. Kodintsev, "Legal Education in the USSR in the Postwar Period," *Legal Education and Science* no. No.2 (2008): 35–39.

A. Ismatov (✉)
Nagoya University, Nagoya, Japan
e-mail: ismatov@law.nagoya-u.ac.jp

M. Kudratov
Regensburg University, Regensburg, Germany
e-mail: manuchehr.kudratov@ur.de

Recently, as a key part of legal education reform, the government initiated large-scale recruitment of legal practitioners to law universities. Inviting practitioners to give lectures to students in the law faculties is not a novelty and has been part of the reform processes in many other former Soviet republics, especially in Central Asia. The main objective of recruiting practitioners is to complement the curriculum, which is usually structured around the theory of law, by incorporating the essential component of the practical implications of the legal profession. What is often missing or omitted when implementing such a policy of large-scale recruitment of legal practitioners as university lecturers is a balance with other vital components of legal education. We argue that teaching law solely through personal legal practice, which is often the case, cannot be successful unless the curriculum ensures the effective integration of two essential components: legal teaching skills and academism. Any significant gaps in either of these components will eventually lead to failure to adequately equip future lawyers with both the required theoretical knowledge and practical skills for the legal profession and in the end will impinge on students' personal motivation to become lawyers. Furthermore, locally educated practitioners whose professional experience mainly covers domestic issues and lacks adequate comparative elements and effective application of concrete case law, are unlikely to be successful in offering solid knowledge or expertise in international law disciplines, such as human rights, international humanitarian law, or international organizations.

In this chapter we will stake stock of recent reforms in legal HE in Uzbekistan. Our research is based on field trips to Uzbekistan in 2019 and 2022 and a series of interviews with legal instructors and undergraduate students at their institutes of higher education.[2] We will draw the reader's attention to the challenges presented by existing curriculum design and teaching methods, and we will argue that too strong an emphasis on practical legal education (by legal practitioners) bears the risk of undermining theoretical legal education as an essential component of legal HE.

Currently, there are four HE institutions in Uzbekistan offering law degrees, including one branch of a foreign university, Westminster International University in Tashkent. This branch is something of a novelty in Uzbekistan's HE system as it is based on a private–public partnership.[3] To date, it is the only foreign HE institution in Uzbekistan which offers LL.B and LL.M degrees with a specific focus on business and commercial law. It was established by the government in 2002 and given the small number of law degree holders has not yet become a competitive player in Uzbekistan's legal HE market. Therefore, our data collection focuses on the two main public universities of Uzbekistan: (1) the University of World Economy and Diplomacy (UWED), particularly its international law faculty, which was created in 1992 in Tashkent with the primary objective of training a new generation of diplomats,

---

[2] A detailed report of the 2022 field trip is published in Aziz Ismatov, *Legal Education in Uzbekistan: Historical Overview and Challenges of Transition*, (CALE Discussion Paper 18, Nagoya, 2019):1–130.
  Consent for republishing excerpts from this report has been obtained from the publisher.

[3] Uzbekistan; Modernizing Tertiary Education (Washington, D.C., 2014).

including international lawyers,[4] and (2) Tashkent State University of Law (TSIL), which was created in 1991 to produce specialists for public services, law enforcement, courts, and administrative bodies.[5] These two public universities occupy a dominant position in the domestic HE market, in terms of their high admission numbers and serving as the main focal points providing access to the legal profession. Hence, focusing on these two HE institutions may provide us with a more comprehensive picture of the contemporary challenges faced by domestic legal education.

2   Postsocialist Curricula Under Revision

There has been very little scholarly debate about the goals of the academic legal curriculum in Uzbekistan. Indeed, this is a phenomenon that many post-Soviet republics have experienced following their post-1990 transition process.[6] In the wake of independence, which, in case of the post-Soviet Central Asian republics came unexpectedly, local legal scholars faced the challenge of having to create an entirely new (nonsocialist) legal system from scratch. This new legal system was expected to ensure the smooth and effective implementation of free market principles instead of those of the planned economy, and the rule of law instead of the socialist legality principle. This was an entirely new undertaking for local lawyers who had been trained according to the socialist law curriculum, had limited knowledge of the specifics of transition, and were, therefore, suddenly faced with unknown challenges they were not prepared for. The process of transition also necessitated creating a new law curriculum, to replace the socialist one, in order to train a new generation of lawyers who would be capable of promoting the aforementioned transition reforms. This new curriculum was also created by the same legal scholars who were trained according to the socialist law curriculum, traditionally known for its overemphasis on the theory of law.

In the 1990s, legal education in Uzbekistan was redesigned, which *inter alia*, presupposed the integration of sociological and practical elements with the theoretical aspects of nonsocialist law. A well-balanced combination of these elements within a legal curriculum could have enabled future lawyers to understand the philosophies of transition and obtain essential skills to move into professional legal practice. In reality, however, the design of the legal curriculum failed to successfully integrate and balance the aforementioned elements and, thus, continued to provide exclusively academic, theoretical education with very little focus on the essence and emerging dilemmas of transition or the practical implications of law. Experts on Western legal

---

[4] *Ukaz Prezidenta Respubliki Uzbekistan 474 o Sozdanii Universiteta Mirovoy Ekonomiki i Diplomatii*, (1992).

[5] *Postanovlenie Kabineta Ministrov pri Prezidente Uzbekskoy SSR N 221 O Preobrazovanii Yuridicheskogo Instituta pri Tashkentskom Gosudarstvennom Universitete im. V. I. Lenina v Tashkentskiy Gosudarstvenniy Yuridicheskiy Universitet*, (1991).

[6] Christopher Waters, *Counsel in The Caucasus: Professionalization And Law In Georgia* (Martinus Nijhoff Publishers, 2004): 38.

education tend to agree that LL.B curricula, which are heavily based on theory and less on practice, do not prepare students for the real world of legal practice.[7] Indeed, for many years, the legal curriculum in Uzbekistan offered students a more sophisticated understanding of law's historical, philosophical, and dogmatic backgrounds. Most of these elements originated in compulsory paralegal subjects, such as the history of state and law, the theory of state and law, Roman law, philosophy, and other disciplines taught during the first and second years of a degree at Soviet Uzbekistan's only law faculty at the Tashkent State University.[8] The mere fact that a degree in law included subjects such as the history and theory of state and law as a key disciplines in the post-1990 law curriculum indicated that a lot had been borrowed from the old Soviet curriculum, which adhered to a doctrine of state-centric theory (and ideology). Furthermore, these disciplines, along with disciplines such as private law or international law which were just beginning to feature on the curricula of Uzbekistan's HE institutions were largely taught by local academics or the so-called "old school" whose academic mindset was established in the context of socialist law.

The current legal curriculum in HE institutions in Uzbekistan has its own particular characteristics. First, it is relatively strict and entails an unreasonably high academic workload. Within four years, students must cover a considerable number of mandatory nonlegal, paralegal, and legal disciplines, and there is not much freedom to specialize in a specific field of law.[9] Second, the core legal courses do not start until the second academic year (in the case of UWED, even the third academic year), while profile legal disciplines mainly feature in the last year of studies. Furthermore, students often have to follow a curriculum that contains a long list of disciplines that are irrelevant to law, with history, mathematics, economics, national ideology, spirituality, ecology, and even IT all appearing on the list of compulsory subjects. A law curriculum of this type cannot, therefore, accommodate students' interests and offer more flexibility in terms of narrowing down the academic focus to a particular discipline or disciplines.

In 2013–14, and most recently in 2017, there were serious and far-reaching attempts to reform the TSUL and UWED legal curricula to reduce the number of mandatory disciplines and encourage a more specific specialization during legal education. This reform could have addressed many issues, thus resulting in a much-awaited transformation of the philosophy of the legal profession from purely dogmatic and dictated by the state to a transition-oriented approach based on academic freedom. The reform of legal education aimed, *inter alia*, at training specialized lawyers with analytical and professional skills to be applied in legal practice, instead of producing traditionally trained lawyers only capable of mechanically applying legal principles. Also, if implemented successfully, this reform could have

---

[7] Also see: J.J. Brunner and A. Tillet, *Higher Education in Central Asia: The Challenges of Modernization: Case Studies from Kazakhstan, Tajikistan, The Kyrgyz Republik, and Uzbekistan.* (Washington, D.C.: World Bank Publications, 2007): 145.

[8] A. F. Shebanov, *Yuridicheskie vyshsie uchebnie zavedenia [Legal Educational Institutes]* (Moscow: Higher School, 1963): 44.

[9] If a student fails to attend a certain percentage of scheduled classes with no valid reason, they are deemed to have failed the course and may be expelled from the university.

paved the way for the emergence of new generation of critical legal elites, including researchers, who would be able to enrich the existing legal academic dogmatism with concrete ideas or solutions to the numerous risks and challenges stemming from the complex process of transition from one legal model to another. As will become evident in the next sections, the reform remains halfhearted and only partially realized, not least because of the difficulties of adapting the law curriculum to the needs of transitional legal education, and the failure to balance essential elements within legal instruction. The following sections will shed more light on such elements and their mixed results.

3 Socratic Teaching Method

Since the TSUL's and UWED's international law faculties were established in the 1990s, their legal training techniques have followed the Soviet style of memorizing black letter law in the form of traditional *ex cathedra* lectures, where only one lecturer teaches a large group of students for 90 min and expects them to memorize long texts.[10] Except for a small minority of professors, lecturers in these institutions still widely adhere to the "top-down" method of teaching domestic law and require students to memorize written law, take lecture notes—*konspekts*—and mechanically apply the codified law in hypothetical cases.[11] The general contents of lectures remain very abstract or purely theoretical, without paying much attention to comparative legal elements and without necessarily initiating an open discussion among students. Furthermore, the lecturer often sticks rigorously to the material assigned for the lecture.[12] If a professor is good enough to keep students focused and interested in the topic, the class can be a very intellectually stimulating session. However, if a lecturer lacks effective communication or speaking skills and does not know how to hold students' attention, the result is often a boring and frustrating monolog where students are no more than physically present. A main point of concern is that teaching law in local universities rarely generates among students critical thinking on practicing law, skills in legal analysis, the ability to absorb a large number of facts and distinguish their relevance, the ability to present arguments appropriately, a thorough understanding of societal and individual problems, and the capacity to develop optimal solutions.

Lecturers rarely explain or provide materials ahead of the next class or encourage students to properly prepare. Therefore, many students often come to class unprepared, negatively impacting their performance and ability to follow the class. Lectures involving repeated memorizing of theoretical concepts are known to be hard to

---

[10] Christopher Waters, *Counsel In The Caucasus: Professionalization And Law In Georgia*, 38;

[11] Kobil Ruziev and Umar Burkhanov, "Uzbekistan: Higher Education Reforms and the Changing Landscape Since Independence," (2018): 444.

[12] Usually by the Ministry of Special Higher and Secondary Education.

concentrate on. The majority of students find such methods monotonous and ultimately fail to adequately understand the course content and retain the theoretical knowledge after graduation.

The most recent educational reforms require cutting back on the number of traditional, top-down lectures. It is intended that under the new scheme, law lecturers will emphasize student-centered learning by relying heavily on the Socratic method of teaching, extensive case law training, and other forms of teaching which encourage students to participate actively and present materials to the class. The core principles and techniques of the Socratic method widely used in Western law schools have raised some concerns among lecturers in Uzbekistan. Notably, the number of adequately trained specialists who can maintain interesting and focus-oriented discussions among students is low. Only a handful of young faculty members who studied abroad sometimes introduce interactive methods, such as class discussions and debates, and note the importance of referring to comparative legal materials which enable students to understand the essence of law, the way it is interpreted, and how it is applied to particular cases.[13] These educators suggest that teaching students how to think like a lawyer would be far more efficient than making them learn theories and doctrines by heart. On the other hand, some lecturers argue that the Socratic method might not always be a good choice as it subjects students with weaker communication skills to a stressful experience. Furthermore, improper application of this method in the class may produce mixed results, neglecting the main topic of the lecture. Some of the senior faculty members who trained in the Soviet system often oppose the initiatives of graduates of foreign universities working in Uzbekistan to introduce the Socratic method as a primary teaching method. In particular, they assert that the Socratic method does not always prove successful in classes with a high number of students or high diversity. Moreover, if, when using such a method, the theory is completely or partially excluded, this does not offer solid knowledge to law students either. Both of these criticisms are sound and deserve closer analysis in light of the prevailing chaotic teaching practice where one of these methods prevails in the class and the another is entirely absent. Educators could bear in mind these valuable critical arguments when designing curricula and ensure that a suitable teaching method is attached to each discipline. This step, if applied in a way that critically reassesses existing teaching practice and its results, which are often revealed in teaching assessments, would strengthen the curriculum and provide it with a sense of logic.

---

[13] For example, by 2019, there were only two of the 20 lecturers at the TSUL with a foreign doctoral degree.

4 Case Law Study

There are also visible problems with the use of case law. In particular, it largely depends on the teacher's expertise and experience in compiling cases. Full-time teachers may create cases independently or copy them from Russian books. Practitioners, on the other hand, may prefer to use cases from their practice.[14] Both methods help students to understand how law is applied in particular circumstances. However, these methods are not very effective when it comes to designing courses for specialized disciplines, such as international law. Indeed, international public law disciplines widely omit any case law element from the curriculum, continuing instead to focus mainly on dogmatic explanations with no reference to the application context.

For example, education on human rights for third-year UWED students integrates, apart from the UN covenants, certain regional human rights treaties, such as the European Convention of Human Rights (ECHR) or the ASEAN Declaration of Human Rights (ADHR). In this class, instructors only provide general knowledge about these treaties, their history, and certain provisions, without going into specifics on the key concepts or the differences between different regional systems. Instructors completely disregard the study of landmark cases, which would enable students to conceptualize, positively or negatively, the spirit of the treaty, the way justices apply the law in each case, to decide on the merits and reparations, and on enforcement. Lecturers also fail to explain the specifics of protection mechanisms that each regional treaty incorporates, or fails to incorporate. As a result, by the end of their studies, most undergraduate students cannot understand the principal difference between the European Court of Human Rights (ECtHR) and the ASEAN Inter-Governmental Commission on Human Rights (AICHR).

Similarly, a comparative law component fleetingly incorporated into specific disciplines, such as constitutional law of foreign states,[15] focuses mainly on the conceptual distinctions between common and civil law, without going into details about how countries that belong to different legal systems address and resolve critical legal issues in their courts. On graduating, it is rare for students to have an adequate understanding and skills in comparative legal methods, simply because it is not a part of the curriculum and, additionally, because certain literature is not referred to, including international cases written mostly in foreign languages.

---

[14] Given the shortage of legal literature in the Uzbek language, Russian-speaking students may have the advantage of being able to refer to Russian law as well if they are lucky to find relevant books in the library or access research data on the web. However, the number of Russian-speaking students is declining annually. According to the 2018 admissions information, of 116 enrolled students, 78 enrolled into classes taught in Uzbek, whereas only 38 registered for Russian-language classes. For more information, see: Aziz Ismatov, *Legal Education in Uzbekistan: Historical Overview and Challenges of Transition*, (CALE Discussion Paper 18, Nagoya, 2019): 58.

[15] Formerly 'Bourgeois Legal Systems'. Refer to, *Law, Studies by Soviet Scholars* (Social Sciences Today Editorial Board, USSR Academy of Sciences, 1985): 141; William Butler, "Soviet International Legal Education: The Pashukanis Syllabus," *Review of Socialist Law* 2 (1976): 80.

Only select mature instructors with a foreign law degree or rich academic and practical experience are in a position to merge theory and practice and refer to foreign laws or cases in their classes. There are just a handful of scholars like this in Uzbekistan who, by drawing on their diverse professional background, successfully incorporate doctrinal, comparative law, and case study methods in their classes. In particular, despite the lack of real legal cases from the national courts, by also relying on the experience gained from active research and involvement in legal reforms in Uzbekistan, these scholars have created a suitable syllabus for their students, containing essential components on theory and practice. These scholars are also trained as teachers, which is another critical aspect of legal education and is reflected in well-structured and well-organized classes. Lecturers like this are the exception. In many other disciplines, lecturers do not have the capacity, for example, to compose a case or appropriately draw on a case from a foreign jurisdiction and demonstrate its applicability in domestic law. Those who refer to cases from other countries tend to limit their focus to a brief overview of the case background, without considering facts, application of the law, merits, and judgment details.[16]

5 Applied Learning

The curriculum that was previously followed in Uzbekistan focused mostly on theoretical aspects of law rather than professional implications. Lack of practical training and awareness of students about professional legal ethics became one of the most serious challenges in Uzbekistan's law universities and urgently required addressing. Therefore, in recent years, the government has decided to place more emphasis on the practical training of law students by recruiting more legal practitioners on a part-time basis to ensure that students are, if not fully, then at least to a certain degree, equipped to perform the tasks assigned to them by their prospective employers.[17]

The primary concern of the present curriculum is the integration of theoretical and doctrinal aspects with practical educational implications. Having realized the significant disconnect between legal education and essential legal practice, local law universities have been struggling to introduce and keep as part of their new curricula several special disciplines fostering the development of practical skills, such as legal academic writing, lawyer's professional speech (or oratory training), legal ethics, legal statistics, system analysis, and personal development. These disciplines encourage students to delve more deeply into a legal working environment. For example, besides its traditional aim of teaching scholarly writing, the legal academic

---

[16] Even disciplines such as EU law and human rights law, which are primarily based on referring to the case law from international courts and tribunals (UN Human Rights Committee, European Court of Justice, European Court of Human Rights), are limited to studying international conventions and statutes.

[17] Postanovlenie Prezidenta Respubliki Uzbekistan (1990), *O Merah po Dal'neyshemu Sovershenstvovaniuy Sistemy Podgotovki Yuridicheskih Kadrov.* (2013). See 9.

writing course at the TSUL additionally aims to teach the skills required for formulating and writing formal complaints to the public, lodging judicial applications, and drafting public–private contracts.[18] Simultaneously, local universities recruit a large number of practitioners of law to teach not only private but also public law. Ultimately this has led to an imbalanced approach where practice-oriented classes have largely replaced theoretical classes.

Indeed, the contents of the courses offered by practitioners are clearly more interactive than traditional lectures. However, in many cases, such courses gradually become more of a regular "sharing of an interesting personal experience" or question–answer session that do not tie the actual practice to the theoretical background.[19] Sometimes, when practitioners share a remarkable experience in dealing with resonance cases, and many students seem to like it, the resulting "active learning sessions" end up making a deep but merely temporary impression. Furthermore, many practitioners lack another vital component essential to the study process: they are not trained legal educators. It is a well-established fact that if even a high-class practitioner who is entirely familiar with the doctrinal aspects of the law lacks essential pedagogical skills, they are unlikely to be successful in transferring their practical knowledge to a younger generation of lawyers.[20]

While a small minority of legal practitioners can combine theory and practice in a well-organized manner, the majority often omit the part on theory and transfer a class into practical storytelling. Furthermore, students reported that many practitioners usually have no chance for regular teaching due to their main job and, therefore, other instructors must replace them.[21] Such a situation eventually leads to mixed-up education and disorientation in the general direction of the class.

6 The Essence of Sociology of Law

A closer look at the state of legal education in Uzbekistan reveals numerous contradictions. Only one aspect of this is described in the present chapter. So what went wrong with or what was missing from the reforms? In the first decade of independence, deeming the Soviet legal education to be ideology oriented and unsuitable

---

[18] Mail correspondence with Deputy Rector Mr. K on the New (Credit) Scheme, 2020. Previously, UWED and TSUL students had a very heavy workload, with some 58 different classes, while under the new modular scheme, they only have 40 modules. Further, the old curriculum presupposed teaching the same courses for all students, regardless of their specialization. Under the new curriculum, all study 26 core subjects then, when they have selected a specialization in a specific direction, for the last two years of their degree, a student can concentrate their own efforts on 14 special subjects of their own personal choice. I think no outsider will understands the difference between modules and subjects here. Could you either shorten this or give examples so that the reader who is entirely unfamiliar with the Uzbek system can understand this explanatory footnote.

[19] Interview, 2019.

[20] Shuvro Sarker, *Legal Education in Asia* (Eleven International Publishing, 2014): 149.

[21] Interview, 2019.

given the realities of the transition from socialism to a market-oriented economy, the government of Uzbekistan decided to distance itself from the existing framework for legal professional education, instead establishing new law faculties with the aim of training "new lawyers". However, by taking a comprehensive look at the core characteristics of post-Soviet legal education, for example, curriculum design, law teaching methods, and general management of relevant HEIs, it is apparent that the legal education system was modeled broadly on the Soviet legal education doctrine and offered no modern sociology of law approaches which would enable students to identify and correctly understand the prevailing contradictions in an Uzbekistan in transition. Here, issues arose, both short and longer term, around producing internationally minded legal scholars and practitioners with intercultural competence, and it eventually affected the trajectory of legal education toward globalization.

A lack of sociology of law incorporated in the law curriculum is one reason why many students fail to understand how vital it was to develop completely new concepts within the context of proposed system transition. Human rights is one of many disciplines that remains poorly conceptualized among students, and even instructors, mainly because of its obscure position and nature within the current process of transition in Uzbekistan. For example, the present Constitution of Uzbekistan (enacted in 1992 and amended several times, with the most fundamental amendments expected by the end of 2022) dedicates Part II to Basic Human and Civil Rights, Freedoms, and Duties. A careful look at the contents of this part of the Constitution reveals that human rights are mainly embodied, not as natural rights, but as citizens' rights and freedoms, which simultaneously stipulate a dichotomy between rights and responsibilities. Article 19 on "The Rights of Citizens" states:

Citizens of the Republic of Uzbekistan and the state shall be bound by mutual rights and mutual responsibility. Citizens' rights and freedoms, established by the Constitution and laws, shall be inalienable. No one shall have the right to deprive or limit them without a court.[22]

Another set of fundamental rights, for example, freedom of thought, speech, and opinion are also guaranteed under the provisions of the current Constitution. However, with the strict control of the media under ex-President Karimov, the exercise of citizens' rights, particularly political freedoms, has often been de facto restricted.[23] The 1992 Constitution abolished the concept of the "dictatorship of the proletariat" and replaced it with the "diversity of political institutions, ideologies, and opinions". Further, the word "human rights", which had been rejected before, was included in the Constitution.

The question of why human rights were introduced in Uzbekistan and the reasons behind the adoption of the new Constitution that included them in the early 1990s can is not easy to answer. One reason for their inclusion may be the rise, after the

---

[22] Article 19, Constitution of the Republic of Uzbekistan (1992).

[23] Also see: John Pottenger, "Civil Society, Religious Freedom, and Islam Karimov: Uzbekistan's Struggle for a Decent Society," *Central Asian Survey 23*, no. 1 (March 1, 2004): 55–77; Pottenger; Zhanna Kozhamberdiyeva, "Freedom of Expression on the Internet: A Case Study of Uzbekistan," *Review of Central and East European Law 33*, no. 1 (January 1, 2008): 95–134.

collapse of the USSR, of anti-socialist reformists promoting political pluralism and calling for the draft Constitution to unconditionally include provisions on human rights. Their radical demands, however, did not meet with full support, as in the process of negotiating the draft Constitution in 1992, conservatives widely opposed the inclusion of human rights as natural rights or *ius naturale*. Eventually, human rights provisions were largely integrated into the category of citizens' rights. In other words, the Constitution still follows a Soviet positivist doctrine according to which rights are granted, and whenever necessary can be limited by the government. Notably, a similar approach is taken not only in the constitutions of other former Soviet states but also in the socialist states of the Association of Southeast Asian Nations (ASEAN) (Vietnam and Laos).

Contemporary human rights theory in Uzbekistan comprises (1) a continuing argument that human rights fall entirely under the state's internal matters; and (2) a strong association with the right to development (of the nation). These notions typically represent a classic example of "Asian human rights" and their close theoretical ties to the third generation of human rights.[24] It subsequently sparked scholarly debates between supporters of the theories of complementarity and those who oppose the third generation of human rights or cultural relativism.[25] The Uzbek government often seeks to approach the human rights concept by actively relying on Asian (oriental) values and the supremacy of national development interests. In this context, the nation-state often uses a rhetoric that justifies the limitation of rights. In particular, in order to achieve developmental goals with specific national characteristics, sacrificing certain freedoms or restricting certain human rights is unavoidable. This focus on development influences the degree of democracy and the rule of law, which in contemporary Uzbekistan is mainly associated with the importance of strong rule by a dominant leader aimed at achieving good results. This conceptual framework, which varies greatly from the Western concept of human rights, is incorporated to the current constitution and public politics in Uzbekistan. It also creates artificial barriers for legal scholars and practitioners to articulate how constitutional provisions on human rights must be created, interpreted, and effectively applied in specific cases. Most importantly, law students cannot conceptualize this state discourse and compare it with other discourses because law curriculums omit the aforementioned crucial element—sociology of law, which would enable students to understand the specifics of post-socialist transition.

---

[24] Tae-Ung Baik, *Emerging Regional Human Rights Systems in Asia* (Cambridge University Press, 2012): 55.

[25] Ibid, 268–69.

7 Conclusion

From a broader historical perspective, the evolution of legal education in Uzbekistan demonstrates two major transitions: from theological to socialist, and from socialist to modern legal education, the latter of which is *de jure* nonsocialist, but in fact, has clear socialist characteristics. The first two decades of the post-Soviet period in Uzbekistan have demonstrated a post-Soviet syndrome frequently seen in the region where law-teaching institutions lag behind the process of transition and remain largely unreformed. New curricula failed to serve as an effective basis for the conceptualization of a new form of legal training and produce a new generation of legal professionals who are able to understand and address the challenges of transition. Simultaneously, the increase in the popularity of law degrees in the context of poorly designed law curriculums and publicly controlled law faculties is a major post-Communist phenomenon, which raises questions about the true essence of legal professions and the tasks which lawyers are expected to perform. There are now many young people who want to obtain a degree in law, motivated by the goal of working as a prosecutor or judge. On the other hand, the profession of lawyer (*advokat*) in Uzbekistan is not as popular as it is, for example, in the Western hemisphere, in Japan, or in Korea. In the developed countries, working as a lawyer is attractive due to the financial stability, freedom, and independence it offers, and the fact that it is not as routine as other public sector jobs. One of many reasons young people in Uzbekistan prioritize working as a prosecutor or law enforcement officer rather than *advokat* is the high level and breadth of the authority of these public institutions. Jobs in the law enforcement sector, an area which has remained totally unchanged since the Soviet era, provide access to considerable administrative resources and involve a far simpler decision-making process as they are able to circumvent many of the usual burdens that make it difficult to address concrete legal issues in Uzbekistan. Perhaps, an independent and more creative, research-based curriculum might encourage young people in Uzbekistan to reconsider their views and approaches toward the legal profession in the future.

The legal education system in today's Uzbekistan is still going through a difficult period of painful transition reforms. Regardless of policymakers' intentions, a small number of universities that teach law have been maintaining formerly socialist curriculums influenced by strong state-centered components. On the other hand, the urgent need to reform legal education has resulted in several attempts to create programs and specializations, as well as to introduce what local educators refer to with the vague term "innovative" teaching technologies. Maintaining this mix of old and new at the same time presents an unresolved challenge, especially when it comes to the theoretical and practical elements of legal education. What has recently been observed is the apparent gravitation of legal education from mainly theoretical settings toward professional legal practice with the wider involvement of nonacademic practitioners. Too much legal practice and a decline in academic training in the education process, in turn, raises serious concerns regarding the traditional philosophy of legal education. Such concerns result from the objective and well-founded fear that too much legal practice can eventually kill off academic legal education. Apart from poorly balanced theoretical and practical compounds, another challenge is the absence of a legal pedagogy component in the process of legal education. This research suggests that legal pedagogy combined in a well-balanced and harmonious way, with legal theory and acceptable practice is an efficient instrument. It would enable graduates of law faculties to acquire skills that would help in offering effective solutions of legal disputes with solid justifications based on a reasonable interpretation and application of laws. The present state of law teaching which specifically aims at giving students the skills to mechanically identify the applicable laws is outdated. Legal education involving all three components to an adequate level would be better suited to training students to continually identify reasons and theoretical justifications for particular laws to be implemented in a particular situation.

Of the several serious concerns mentioned in this chapter, another crucial one is the adaptation of case study law for the legal curriculum. While studying law based on analyzing concrete and relevant cases has proven to be successful in many countries, it is not yet clear how this method will pan out in Uzbekistan, a country with no rich and valuable legal practice material to serve as a basis for studying case law. In very exceptional or limited circumstances, a handful of law instructors, relying on their own considerable experience and potential, may be able to reconstruct available or create new cases, and successfully integrate these into course curricula. In reality, however, the majority of law instructors in Uzbekistan do not have this kind of experience and simply cannot conceptualize the idea of a successful case study doctrine. While utilizing a case study method, instructors could add a comparative element to demonstrate how law can be similarly or differently applied in contextual cases in foreign jurisdictions. This type of method would help students not only to understand foreign law, but primarily to conceptualize their own legal system and its specific features. Further, when comparing case studies, explanations for numerous conflicts with local law, would expand students' horizons regarding the hybrid nature of the legal system. Apart from the old socialist law and current nonsocialist black letter law, Uzbekistan's law is also based on strong traditional elements originating from its specific culture and history, which influence the whole process of legal interpretation and application in the country. This approach requires not only legal but also adequate linguistic skills.

Presently, legal research in Uzbekistan is stagnant and certain changes are required to revitalize it. A further increase in academic freedom and greater interest in supporting legal research from both public and non-public stakeholders may pave the way for such reinvigoration and contribute to advancing the philosophy of law and law education in Uzbekistan. Conceptualization of law is another serious missing component. Imported disciplines, such as legal ethics, sociology of law, lawyers' professional responsibility, comparative legal research, and analysis, cannot make any kind of substantial contribution to a successful curriculum unless they are well-conceptualized and enable students to identify legal contradictions occurring in contemporary Uzbekistan. In this regard, comparative law should not be aimed at simply transplanting foreign laws, as is currently the case, but must enable professionals to understand laws in a comparative perspective with foreign systems and create norms by paying due attention to the local characteristics and requirements of their own society. Simultaneously, lawyers must bear in mind that universal norms, such as human rights, do not always coexist with local culture and society. This is a common phenomenon in Asia, which, since the end of the Cold War, has become a serious concern regarding the applicability of human rights as a Western product imported into the local non-Western context. This complex paradox is also rooted in the current legal education system's weak approach to the philosophies of human rights and their ineffective dissemination among future lawyers. Legal educators in the transition societies of wider Central Asia, therefore, need to consider how, apart from being normatively transplanted into the constitutional text, practice-based case study law on human rights with domestic and foreign comparative elements may emerge as an effective tool to educate future lawyers.

References

Baik T (2012) Emerging regional human rights systems in Asia. Cambridge University Press, Cambridge

Brunner J, Tillet A (2007) Higher education in Central Asia: the challenges of modernization: case studies from Kazakhstan, Tajikistan, The Kyrgyz Republic, and Uzbekistan. World Bank Publications, Washington, D.C.

Butler W (1976) Soviet international legal education: the pashukanis syllabus. Rev Soc Law 2:80

Christopher W (2004) Counsel in the caucasus: professionalization and law in Georgia. Martinus Nijhoff Publishers, Leiden, p 38

Constitution of the Republic of Uzbekistan (1992)

Ismatov A (2019) Legal education in Uzbekistan: historical overview and challenges of transition. CALE Discussion Paper 18

Kodintsev A (2008) Legal education in the USSR in the postwar period. Legal Educ Sci 2:35–39

Kozhamberdiyeva Z (2008) Freedom of expression on the internet: a case study of Uzbekistan. Rev Central East Euro Law 33(1):95–134

Law studies by soviet scholars. social sciences today editorial board. USSR Acad Sci

Postanovlenie Kabineta Ministrov pri Prezidente Uzbekskoy SSR N 221 O Preobrazovanii Yuridicheskogo Instituta pri Tashkentskom Gosudarstvennom Universitete im. V. I. Lenina v Tashkentskiy Gosudarstvenniy Yuridicheskiy Universitet [Order of the Cabinet of Ministers under the President of the Republic of Uzbekistan N 221 regarding the transformation of the Law Institute under the Tashkent State University named after V. I. Lenin into the Tashkent State Institute of Law] (1991)

Postanovlenie Prezidenta Respubliki Uzbekistan 1990, O Merah po Dal'neyshemu Sovershenstvovaniuy Sistemy Podgotovki Yuridicheskih Kadrov [Order of the President of the Republic of Uzbekistan N 1990 on measures towards further improvement of the training system of legal cadres] (2013).

Pottenger J (2004) Civil society, religious freedom, and Islam Karimov: Uzbekistan's struggle for a decent society. Central Asian Surv 23(1):55–77

Ruziev K, Burkhanov U (2018) Uzbekistan: higher education reforms and the changing landscape since independence. In: Huisman J et al (ed) 25 years of transformations of higher education systems in post-soviet Countries. Palgrave Macmillan, Cham

Sarker S (2014) Legal education in Asia. Eleven International Publishing, Den Haag, p 149

Shebanov AF (1963) Yuridicheskie vyshsie uchebnie zavedenia [Legal Educational Institutes]. Higher School, Moscow, p 44

Ukaz Prezidenta Respubliki Uzbekistan 474 o Sozdanii Universiteta Mirovoy Ekonomiki i Diplomatii [Resolution of the President of the Republic of Uzbekistan on the establishment of the university of World Economy and Diplomacy], (1992)

World Bank, Uzbekistan; Modernizing Tertiary Education, the World Bank Report, Washington, D.C., 2014. Accessed via https://www.worldbank.org/content/dam/Worldbank/document/eca/central-asia/Uzbekistan-Higher-Education-Report-2014-en.pdf. Last Accessed 20 Dec 2020

Open Access This chapter is licensed under the terms of the Creative Commons Attribution 4.0 International License (http://creativecommons.org/licenses/by/4.0/), which permits use, sharing, adaptation, distribution and reproduction in any medium or format, as long as you give appropriate credit to the original author(s) and the source, provide a link to the Creative Commons license and indicate if changes were made.

The images or other third party material in this chapter are included in the chapter's Creative Commons license, unless indicated otherwise in a credit line to the material. If material is not included in the chapter's Creative Commons license and your intended use is not permitted by statutory regulation or exceeds the permitted use, you will need to obtain permission directly from the copyright holder.

Inclusive Human Rights Education in Tajikistan

Mohirakhoni Husnidinzoda

1 Introduction

> There needs to be a lot more emphasis on what a child can do instead of the conventional wisdom of what [she or] he can't do.
>
> Temple Grandin[1]

During Soviet times, education for disabled children had always been segregated, the vestiges of which remained after Central Asian states became independent in 1991. Tajikistan is one case study of many, which illustrates how, depending on the severity of the disability, children were placed in various types of special schools. The "science of defectology", which integrated components of psychology, medicine, and pedagogy, was used to develop special education. Soviet defectology viewed a child with a disability as defective and in need of medical treatment and lifelong care. The branch evolved as an unclear, "occupationally ambiguous therapeutic field" for children considered "difficult to treat", "difficult to teach", and "difficult to discipline". Segregated education was implemented throughout the Soviet Socialist Republics, placing pupils with disabilities in self-contained classrooms, which not only isolated them from society, but also "ensured that their isolation would be permanent in most cases" (20). Since the collapse of the Soviet Union, many former Soviet republics have continued to pursue a policy of segregation, placing people with impairments in residential care institutions (Gevorgianiene and Sumskiene 2017).

Today, according to Wang (2009), the segregation of disabled children from mainstream education, as well as economic and social activities, is significantly higher in economically less developed countries. In the context of the five post-Soviet Central

---

[1] Quoted in Stubbs 2008, p. 31.

M. Husnidinzoda (✉)
Civic Education and Critical Thinking, Khujand, Tajikistan
e-mail: m.husnidinzoda@osce-academy.net

© The Author(s) 2023
A. Mihr and C. Wittke (eds.), *Human Rights Dissemination in Central Asia*, SpringerBriefs in Political Science,
https://doi.org/10.1007/978-3-031-27972-0_7

Asian states of Kazakhstan, Kyrgyzstan, Tajikistan, Turkmenistan, and Uzbekistan, issues around limited access to education for children with special needs have not been given much attention. The newly independent postcommunist governments have been heavily influenced by the Soviet legacy, characterized by a special "correctional approach" and segregation when dealing with children with special needs. That said, the problems associated with educational exclusion and the rights of children with special needs to quality education are increasingly on the agendas of policymakers worldwide, with many developed and developing countries (including in the post-Soviet space) adopting the concept of IE (Bines and Lei 2011: 420). The introduction and adoption of the concept in the laws of many post-Soviet states began between 2008 and 2010. As a result, children with special needs were granted the right, at least in formal terms if not in practice, to study in regular schools (Gevorgianiene and Sumskiene 2017).

An interview with an education specialist working for the United Nations Children's Fund (UNICEF) in Tajikistan in 2021 revealed that over several decades, the situation regarding disabled children's access to quality education had supposedly improved and become more of a priority in the Tajik government's education agenda. In the past children with special needs would have attended special schools. More recently, however, the inclusion of children with disabilities in mainstream education, claims the specialist, has become an agenda item for the Tajik authorities.[2]

Nonetheless, non-governmental organizations (NGOs), such as Save the Children, ranked Tajikistan 99th out of 180 countries surveyed in its 2020 "End of Childhood Index", highlighting serious threats to children's well-being and measuring the effects of other factors such as "ill health, malnutrition, exclusion from education, child labor, child marriage, early pregnancy, conflict, and extreme violence", giving the country the worst score of all postcommunist countries in the post-Soviet space and the broader region of Eastern Europe (Save the Children 2020). A recent UNICEF report indicates that despite the Tajik government's supposed attempt to provide equal educational opportunities to children with special needs and children with disabilities (CwD), the vast majority of CwD remain excluded from quality education. Of the estimated 150,000 people with disabilities in Tajikistan, approximately 26,000 are children and a high percentage are young people ages 15 to 24 who are not in education, employment, or training. On the local level, the situation varies widely across the country. Overall, however, it indicates a tremendous waste of human potential in Tajikistan (UNICEF 2019).

Considering the aforementioned and bearing in mind the importance of issues pertaining to education for children with special needs, and especially the need for broad awareness of these issues in Tajik civil society and society in general, this chapter aims to provide a critical overview of the current situation in the development and implementation of IE for children with special needs in Tajikistan, and to assess improvements (or lack thereof) in recent years. It also examines the remaining gaps

---

[2] Interview with Shahnoz Valijonbekova, UNICEF education specialist, Dushanbe, 10 June 2021, Dushanbe (via Zoom).

in the relevant legislation and government programs, as well as societal perceptions of the issue of IE.

2 Development of Inclusive Education

Muhammadieva (2002: 6) claims that on paper, the Republic of Tajikistan recognizes that a mentally or physically disabled child should live a full and decent life in conditions that "ensure dignity, promote self-reliance, and facilitate the child's active participation in the community", as stated in Article 23 of the United Nations Convention on the Rights of the Child (UNCRC), which Tajikistan ratified in 1993 (UNCRC 1990). While the definition of "disability" according to the UN Convention on the Rights of Persons with Disabilities (UNCRPD) is based on the social model and stated as follows:

> Persons with disabilities include those who have long-term physical, mental, intellectual or sensory impairments which in interaction with various barriers may hinder their full and effective participation in society on an equal basis with others (UNCRPD 2006: 2)

The definition in Article 1 of Tajikistan's Law on Social Protection of Persons with Disabilities is based on the medical model and defines an "invalid" as a person whose.

> health is damaged due to long-term impairments caused by impairment of body functions, complex illnesses, trauma, physical and intellectual defects resulting in limited ability to carry out day-to-day tasks and leading to the need for social support (IPHR 2018: 17)

By definition, a child's disability is a long-term "social maladjustment" caused by a "chronic disease" or "pathological condition" that severely limits their capacity to integrate into an environment appropriate for their age (6). Disabled children require constant and special care, which is supposed to be provided by the state through Tajikistan's Ministries of Public Health, Labor and Social Protection, and Education. There are also a number of NGOs that deal with issues affecting disabled children, focusing on the protection of children's rights, as well as the "rehabilitation and socioeconomic support" of disabled children, largely through foreign-funded projects and programs. The Ministry of Public Health is usually in charge of putting together the list of "medical and social indications and counter-indications" for placing children with physical or mental developmental handicaps in a children's home, special children's preschool institutions, residential schools, or residential homes for children with different disabilities (Aiyubova 2013: 7).

In sum, Tajikistan has long used separate and segregated school systems for healthy children and CwD. Special schools for CwD have been established, which have both advantages and disadvantages. Due to issues such as a lack of special educational facilities and the inability to enroll all disabled children in special secondary schools based on their physical disabilities, as well as a lack of favorable conditions and access to quality education in special and boarding schools, in addition to massive lobbying by child rights advocates, the Tajik government may have been compelled by law to create favorable conditions for disabled children to study at the same level with children with no disability. Eventually, the Tajik government decided to move away from the segregated system inherited from Soviet "defectology" toward an inclusive educational system where children with and without disabilities are placed in regular general secondary schools, as a means of integration of children with disabilities into society (Aiyubova 2013).

The regulation on inclusive education is now included in Tajik legislation such as the Law on Education of the Republic of Tajikistan (2013) and the National Strategy for Education Development (2006–2015), and the National Concept of Inclusive Education for CwD (2011–2015), authorized by President Rahmon. The latter conceptual framework was developed to make it possible to provide the conditions necessary for children with disabilities to get an education in kindergartens and regular schools, allowing them to exercise their rights to a quality education with minimal restrictions. The framework outlined the strategy for implementing IE, as well as the objectives and expected outcomes (Aiyubova 2013).

3 Legislation on Inclusive Education

The Tajik government's education policy aims to drastically alter the education system by drafting and supposedly implementing several laws and regulations governing the country's educational system. The Republic's highest levels of government claim to be supportive of initiatives to build and improve on IE (GoT 2011). The right to education is guaranteed in the 1994 Constitution of Tajikistan, which was amended in 2003 and now states: "Everyone shall have the right to education…" (Article 41). The Constitution obliges the government to provide free basic education, general vocational education, primary special education, vocational special education, and higher special education in public schools. The nondiscrimination provision guarantees equal rights and freedoms "regardless of nationality, color, sex, language, religious beliefs, political affiliation, knowledge, social, or property status" (Article 17). In terms of specific groups, in Article 34, the Constitution ensures that orphans and CwD are protected and educated (GoT 1994).

The 2011–2015 National Framework for IE for CwD was developed by a working group within the Ministry of Education and Science, which included representatives of different agencies and NGOs with the aim of developing an IE system from preschool to general education to enforce the rights of all children and young people to quality education "with minimal restrictions". The National Strategy for Education Development (2006–2015) had aimed to create an appropriate system for early detection and correction. It had continued to support special education, in part by "improving interministerial cooperation for the education, rehabilitation, and socialization" of CwD.

The 2013 Law on Education defines IE as the creation of favorable conditions for children in education regardless of "gender, race, language, nationality, religious beliefs, physical or mental disabilities, abilities, cultural and social status" (Article 1). The law guarantees inclusivity of education for various vulnerable groups, and special education for CwD. To do this, special educational establishments, which provide particular conditions tailored to the children's needs and special education programs, as well as medical and social rehabilitation, are supposed to be created throughout the country.

The United Nations Educational, Scientific and Cultural Organization (UNESCO) and its Global Education Monitoring Report (2021) highlight that although the Tajik legal system does not explicitly promote an exclusively IE system, it does provide the legal underpinning for its implementation, in accordance with the 2013 Law on Education (UN Commission on Human Rights 1990, UN SDG GA 2015, UNESCO 2008, UNESCO 2017, UNICEF 2017). All children and young people, including those with disabilities, have the right to an education under the Law on Education (Article 16.5). However, the law stipulates that children with disabilities who are unable to attend ordinary schools must be educated in special education institutions (Article 22.3). As a result, the law "preserves elements of the medical and defectology approaches" by concentrating on limitations to identify a disability.

According to the International Partnership for Human Rights (IPHR) (2018), Tajikistan's National Development Strategy up to 2030 considers IE a crucial indicator for the quality improvement of the education system. The objective of implementing IE and developing a system capable of responding to students' specific needs, particularly those at risk of exclusion, is also indicated in this national strategy. However, the IPHR report also points out that there is no publicly available information on the activities implemented in relation to PwD under numerous national programs. Some parts of the National Program for the Rehabilitation of Invalids, for example, were labeled "pending international funding", and no information about the budgetary resources spent or allocated for this program were publicly available, making it impossible to determine which plans have been implemented let alone evaluate them (13).

Furthermore, the analysis of the Tajikistan's legal norms in the field of education and the Law on the Social Protection of Persons with Disabilities, conducted by the IPHR (2018) discovered a "lack of regulation and consistency for the learning process of PwD, particularly children with various types of disabilities". According to this report, there is no clear outline of the curriculum for children with visual impairments or hearing difficulties in general education. There is also no clear vision of the conditions that must be provided for these children.

Another shortcoming in legislation pertaining to issues around the inclusion of PwD and CwD indicated by IPHR is "the declarativeness of rights and guarantees of inclusion and lack of enforcing mechanisms of these guarantees", which are evidenced by the IPHR's analysis of government standards in various forms of education. One such mechanism was in fact put in place in Tajikistan with the adoption of the 2011–2015 National Concept of IE, which also lacked monitoring for phases that have been implemented (15). The Ministry of Education and Science did not report whether the first stage of the concept's implementation had been completed or when the second is expected to begin, which indicates the inadequate attention paid to the proper development of Tajikistan's education system as a whole and for CwD, in particular.

To date, developmentally impaired children have mainly attended special institutions and boarding schools (for children with impaired hearing, vision, speech, and motor skills or for children with intellectual and learning disabilities). In Tajikistan, the results-oriented inclusion of developmentally challenged children in a regular school environment is carried out on a case-by-case basis, taking into account individual factors and experiences (IPHR 2018). To provide the conditions necessary for exercising basic educational and social rights, Tajikistan provides consultations for children with suspected developmental impairments conducted by "psychological, medical, and pedagogical commissions" (PMPCs) in the cities of Dushanbe, Khujand, and Isfara (in the northern Sughd province) and Qurghonteppa (southern Khatlon province). The PMPC services are supposedly provided by a wide range of "practitioners from different professions" including social workers, specialists on visual and/or hearing impairments, and experts in developmental disabilities. The main goal of this type of commission is to examine children under the age of 18 to assess and diagnose any particular developmental needs early on, as well as to determine the curriculum, methods, and type of schooling that will best fit each child's specific needs. Based on the diagnosis, PMPCs recommend an education placement, which may include assigning children to boarding schools, mainstream schools, or homeschooling under the supervision of a local institution should there be a lack of accessible infrastructure (IPHR 2018: 18).

4 Shortcomings in Inclusive and Human Rights Education

According to a UNICEF report (2019), many children in the early years of life in Tajikistan, particularly CwD, are still denied access to quality education and early childhood development services. There is also a shortage of trustworthy data on CwD, since there is no suitable data collection mechanism in place. For example, according to the Ministry of Health and Social Protection, there are over 28,000 children with impairments, but this number only includes those children who are registered and receive a disability allowance. Despite the fact that Tajikistan ratified the UNCRPD in 2018 and the UNCRC in 1993, the country has failed to make even the smallest of steps toward fulfilling these commitments. In Article 24 (Education) of the Convention on the Rights of Persons with Disabilities it states:

> States Parties recognize the right of persons with disabilities to education. With a view to realizing this right without discrimination and on the basis of equal opportunity, States Parties shall ensure an inclusive education system at all levels and lifelong learning directed to:
>
> a. The full development of human potential and sense of dignity and self-worth, and the strengthening of respect for human rights, fundamental freedoms and human diversity;
>
> b. The development by persons with disabilities of their personality, talents and creativity, as well as their mental and physical abilities, to their fullest potential (UNCRPD 2006 Optional Protocol: 16).

Nevertheless, all children in Tajikistan are denied learner-centered teaching and learning due to the country's knowledge-based system that lacks child-friendly facilities and suffers from a shortage of qualified teachers and educational materials. The government has supposedly begun curricular reform to improve the quality of education and learning outcomes for all children. However, current professional conventions based on a medical model of disability, in which CwD are considered better served in institutions with specialized medical support, are impeding further progress in the integration of children with disabilities at the community level. Additionally, according to a UNICEF report (2019), Tajikistan also lacks a learning assessment system, and learning outcomes are not consistently measured. This means that educational reforms are based on unreliable or no data at all, and recent examinations have shown that early grade reading skills and comprehension are poor.

According to the concluding observations of a report by the UN Committee on the Rights of the Child (2017) on the report Tajikistan is required to submit to the Committee, serious concerns are raised about the inadequate protection of children with disabilities from discrimination. The Committee particularly indicates the following shortcomings: "(a) Shortage of reliable data, which hinders the delivery and evaluation of services for children with disabilities; (b) Continued limited physical accessibility of public institutions, transportation and housing; (c) Limited availability of State-funded early detection and diagnosis of disability and rehabilitation services; (d) Absence of a comprehensive approach to the needs of children with disabilities and their families, and particularly to the needs of adolescent girls with disabilities; (e) Insufficient social welfare allowances and services provided to children with disabilities with high needs and their families that do not sufficiently encourage and provide support for families to keep their children at home, resulting in a disproportionate number of children with disabilities continuing to live in institutions; (f) Extremely limited access to quality education for children with disabilities" (7).

In light of the serious concerns raised above, the UN Committee repeats its previous recommendation and urges Tajikistan to adopt a human rights-based approach to disability and to develop a "comprehensive strategy" for the inclusion of children with disabilities (7).

Based on my personal empirical observations and anecdotal evidence, despite the work that has been done by the government, there are several serious issues with the way Tajikistan's educational institutions operate. Among other things, there are still not enough preschool facilities and regular schools in the country that are capable of implementing IE for CwD. Neither specialized institutions nor general schools have enough and/or qualified psychological/medical/pedagogical advisors. There are also not enough developmental disability specialists, such as teachers for the hearing impaired and speech impaired. Moreover, one of the determining factors in providing comprehensive support for disabled children is taking preventive measures designed to lower health risks to newborns and infants. In Tajikistan, most women and adolescents do not have access to healthcare and do not receive medical treatment (IPHR 2018). People are unable to get checkups because there are not enough medical services, especially in rural areas. A major obstacle to the implementation of IE in Tajikistan is the public's lack of awareness, which sees children with developmental disabilities being excluded or ignored and subject to social stigma throughout the country despite the lobbying efforts of numerous NGOs (Gevorgianiene and Sumskiene 2017).

In addition to what has already been mentioned, UNESCO and GEM (2021) identified problems associated with learning environments, particularly in terms of infrastructure, as well as curriculum and teaching and support personnel, as obstacles to the successful inclusion of CwDs in Tajikistan. Though state authorities are required to regulate the building of barrier-free social infrastructure, including educational institutions and amenities and transportation services, as specified in the 2010 Law on Social Protection of Persons with Disabilities (Article 25), most existing infrastructure in Tajikistan is still not accessible for PwD.

5 The Virtual Nature of Inclusive Education

The Tajik government's advocacy for the rights of disabled people, including children, is in fact far more "virtual" than real. Despite the government's avowed attempt to provide quality educational opportunities to all CwD and to pursue a policy of IE, the form of IE that currently exists in Tajikistan is reduced to nominal integration of children with special needs in mainstream education, with almost no environmental (physical, visual, and auditory) and curriculum adaptation for CwD.

To test the aforementioned claim that the Tajik government's advocacy for IE is only of a virtual nature and integrated and inclusive education are conflated, a range of in-depth semi-structured interview questions were created that included five categories of people directly involved in the topic under examination, such as (i) heads of local NGOs or their representatives ($N = 4$) that claim to promote IE in Tajikistan; (ii) school principals or teachers who teach CwD in mainstream schools in Sughd province ($N = 6$); (iii) parents of CwD who have had a positive or negative experience with the inclusion of their children in education as well as the children themselves ($N = 10$); (iv) human rights experts and education specialists working for international organizations (IOs) in the fields of CwD and PwD inclusion in education ($N = 4$); and (v) government officials in the State Committee on Children's Rights and in the Sughd provincial Ministry of Education ($N = 4$). Of the number of respondents indicated, 20 (or 71%) agreed to be interviewed. These interlocutors were in the cities of Khujand and Dushanbe, and the northern Sughd districts of Chashma, and Bobojon Ghafurov. The interviews were conducted via whichever mode was preferred by the respondent and practical for both the respondent and myself. Nine were conducted in person, four via Zoom, and seven by phone. To analyze whether or not the concepts of inclusion and integration of CwD are muddled in Tajik educational practice, I benchmarked universally agreed standards for IE and the definition of IE according to the UNCRPD and the UNESCO Salamanca Statement that state "recognition of the need to work toward 'schools for all'—institutions which include everybody, celebrate differences, support learning, and respond to individual needs regardless of differences or disabilities" (UNESCO 1994: 14). I thus begin testing my argument by looking at the definitions and perceptions of IE among my interviewees.

6 Perceptions and Misperceptions

While defining the concept of IE, those of my interlocutors representing families with disabled children, teachers, and school principals unanimously highlighted the right of every child to be educated at general mainstream schools together with children without disabilities (GoT 1994). However, limited attention was paid to the need to provide access to quality education with the conditions necessary to accommodate the needs of every learner (GoT 2011, GoT 2016, IPHR 2017). For instance, when defining the concept of IE, Madinakhon Sulaimonova (not her real name), a secondary school teacher who teaches children with disabilities, responded that, for her, "IE means all children have the right to study together at general educational institutions."[3] Similarly, the right of CwD to be educated in mainstream schools was repeatedly stated by other schoolteachers and some parents of CwD. The responses of the UNICEF education specialist I spoke to as well as representatives of the "Iroda" and "Ranginkamon" NGOs indicated perceptions of IE that were more comprehensive and resonated with the universal understanding of what inclusion means. According to the UNICEF specialist, Shahnoz Valijonbekova, IE means "quality education adapted to the needs of each and everyone, regardless of her/his status, religious beliefs, ethnicity and abilities".[4] According to this expert, in practice, IE has characteristics of integration in education because until recently, inclusion of children in Tajikistan's general secondary schools was primarily advocated, promoted, and requested by parents of CwD and parent associations. This resulted in a significant demand for IE, prompting the Tajik government to pay more attention to the issue and recognize the need to take measures in an effort to provide quality inclusive education for CwD.

In recent years, international policy and underlying views of disability have shifted from being based on the "medical" to the "social" model in much of the world. Reiser (2012), in turn, describes the disability movement's influence on education as "the hammer" which met "the anvil" of parents' desire for their children to be part of the local community (23). Perhaps there was a similar movement in Tajikistan which prompted the government to adopt IE policy—albeit one whose effectiveness is questioned by the interlocutors interviewed for this study.

The abovementioned UNICEF specialist, for example, stated: "our country lacks the vision of how to transform the system to fulfill the required criteria of inclusivity [for CwD] and lacks a strategic plan of action" when putting this concept into

---

[3] Interview with Madinakhon Sulaimonova, Tajik language teacher, Secondary School #5, Khujand, in-person interview, 13 September 2021.

[4] Interview with Valijonbekova, *op. cit.*

practice.[5] Additionally, the head of the NGO "Ranginkamon" (Rainbow), Baroat Aminova (not her real name), argued:

> Although we have adopted a national concept of IE that focuses on integrating most children with physical disabilities, what practice shows us is that the policy lacks clear mechanisms for a stage-by-stage implementation; [the reality is that] in our country, IE implementation and initiatives happen in a chaotic manner.[6]

She further commented that even when CwD is accepted in schools, after just two or three months, parents are usually advised by school officials to transfer their children to special schools, informing them: "Your child's abilities don't fit our school's curriculum."[7]

Given the above responses and other evidence, it appears that the existing form of inclusion implemented throughout Tajikistan's secondary schools is reduced to nominal integration of those disabled children with the type of physical disability that makes integration easier, whereas children with intellectual disabilities are directed to boarding schools after taking into account the diagnoses of psychological, medical, pedagogical advice (PMPC). In one of the interviews, a representative of the NGO "Nazari Digar" (Alternative) highlighted that children with Down syndrome are often not accepted in mainstream schools even when a parent can provide PMPC approval for their child to be educated at a general school. Schools justify this rejection by stating that "the school staff don't know how to work with such children whereas specialists in boarding schools can meet the child's special educational needs."[8] In some cases parents are asked to provide an "approval statement from psychiatric hospitals" as well as from the PMPC to demonstrate that the child can be educated. Such attitudes discourage parents from sending their children to secondary schools where their child will probably not be supported or accepted for who they are. According to one mother of a child with Down syndrome, "I was told that studying at a mainstream school wouldn't benefit my child as she has a mental impairment and wouldn't be able to follow a learning program."[9] It is not unusual for parents to receive such recommendations from schools and very often even those whose children have only mild intellectual disabilities are discouraged from sending them to general schools with the argument that the children's needs are best served by specialists in boarding schools.

Despite evidence of the damage institutionalization inflicts on children, many professionals in Tajikistan still seem to favor institution-based special education over community-based IE. The inefficiency of the institutions and poor functioning

---

[5] *Ibid.*

[6] Interview with Baroat Aminova, Director of NGO "Ranginkamon", Khujand, phone interview, 7 August 2021.

[7] *Ibid.*

[8] Interview with Parvinakhon Mahmudova, NGO worker, "Nazari Digar" (Alternative), Khujand, in-person interview, 25 June 2021.

[9] Interview with Shanozakhon Sharipova, mother of child with Down syndrome, Khujand, phone interview, 10 July 2021.

of the model in practice in Tajikistan are also highlighted in a report by the NGO "Ishtirok" which indicates that.

> ....the PMPC [in many districts of the country] fail with their structure of psychologists, speech therapists, and other professionals to provide quality services. Most 'comprehensive' schools are not able to provide the suitable infrastructure for schoolchildren with disabilities (ramps, elevators, toilets) or training for children with special needs, since there are not enough teachers who know sign language or Braille. There are no special programs for such students, nor are there enough tutors to support such children ..." (ASPBAE and Ishtirok 2018: 17)

Even when children with mild intellectual or physical disabilities are accepted in mainstream schools, they are not provided with a quality education, because the school curriculum is not adapted to the child's individual needs, school educators are not given sufficient training and are not equipped to teach CwD and schools do not have the accessible infrastructure. Parents themselves acknowledge the fact that while attending mainstream schools, their children gain socializing skills, but little else.

7 The Policy-Implementation Gap

For sidewalks, transport and public and private buildings including schools, dormitories, medical institutions, and places of work, Tajikistan's Law on Social Protection of Persons with Disabilities, Article 25, paragraph 4, obliges the state to provide access to persons with disabilities to relevant institutions and social infrastructure, in addition to transport services (GoT 2010). Organizations providing transport services to the public are obliged to equip buses and vehicles, bus stops, bus stations, airports, and other places with facilities to make them accessible to PwD, claims the law. In reality, however, the law is not upheld and such rules and regulations are practically never enforced.

There is a clear shortage of highly qualified professionals to work with CwD in schools, and provide psychological, medical, and pedagogical consultations, despite the fact that the government's IE policy for 2011–2015 outlines the necessity of training specialists. One of the reasons for the shortage is the absence in Tajikistan's higher education institutions and education institutes of further training and study programs for special education and psychology geared toward IE (Save the Children 2016). There are virtually no specialists in these disciplines. Scientific and methodological approaches to the issues around the early stages of development and education of children with intellectual and physical disabilities are not developed in existing state institutions, such as in the Academy of Education.

In addition, the needs of CwD are not taken into account in the education standards of preschool and general secondary education, despite several supposed program revisions. As the interview with Dilfuza Hodiboeva (not her real name), a teacher in Khujand, revealed, children with and without disabilities, in her experience, follow the same learning program approved by the Ministry of Education and the same school curriculum, which has not changed since Hodiboeva's school began accepting CwD in 2018. Moreover, she believes that IE within the current system only benefits children with mild physical disabilities, thus leaving the majority of CwD to attend boarding schools.[10] "The failure by the government to provide inclusive education or appropriate education for CwD living in specialized institutions breaches the UN [Convention on the Rights of the Child]" (Jones 2002: 8). The Tajik government fails to comply with these obligations as it has still not developed a proper functioning policy and strategy to implement IE for CwD. There is thus s significant policy-implementation gap when it comes to IE in Tajikistan.

8 Unclear Inclusive Education Assessment System

The existing system of education for children in Tajikistan lacks a learning assessment system meaning that learning outcomes are not consistently measured. As a result, educational reforms are not based on systematic data, and school examinations have shown that early-grade reading skills and comprehension are poor, especially among CwD. According to Zulaikho Rahimova (not her real name), a teacher in Khujand, CwD are often taught the bare minimum from the curriculum, and they often fail their school exams, but still move on to the next level of instruction, supposedly to avoid discouraging or demotivating them from studying. The same interlocutor saw the goal of the IE learning program for CwD as an opportunity "to teach CwD the basic necessary knowledge and the social skills that they would need to interact with others in adulthood".[11]

Another example that illustrates the shortcomings mentioned above is that society's widespread response to disability and attitude toward disabled persons in Tajikistan is one of compassion and charity. During the period of research, several schoolteachers stated that it is difficult for CwD to keep up with the lesson in a classroom of 35–40 pupils and therefore some teachers work individually with CwD after classes without compensation for the sake of "*savob*" (reward from God) and "*uvol*" (compassion). As a result of such attitudes—despite the good intentions of such educators—disabled people in Tajikistan are typically viewed as victims in need of social protection, rather than as active participants with full rights equal to those of any other member of society. According to Sabohat Hakimzoda, the director of an NGO, although work is being done at the local level by civil society organizations to shift disability issues toward a social-legal model based on human rights, the Soviet

---

[10] Interview with Dilfuza Hodiboeva, teacher, secondary school #7, Khujand, in-person interview, 20 September 2021.

[11] Interview with Zulaikho Rahimova, teacher, secondary school #4, Khujand, in-person interview, 14 September 2021.

legacy of the medical model still prevails in the perceptions of as much as 80% of the Tajik population.[12]

9 Conclusion

The exclusion of children with disabilities from education has long been based on misconceptions about their ability to benefit from and participate fully in education. Historically, worldwide, efforts to educate CwD relied on separate schools, with particular impairments being specifically targeted in specialized institutions. Such institutions served only a small percentage of those in need and were therefore found to be inefficient. In a context of violations of the rights of PwD/CwD and their stigmatization by societies, the need for a rights-based approach toward education for CwD arose and the concept of inclusive education emerged for the first time in general guarantees set forth in the UN's 1948 Universal Declaration on Human Rights. Much later, this was reaffirmed more forcefully by the 1990 World Declaration on Education for All, and in more detailed form in the UNESCO's (1994) Salamanca Statement on Principles, Policies and Practice in Special Needs Education and lastly in the 2008 Convention on the Rights of Persons with Disabilities.

Inclusive education aims for all children, with and without disabilities, to learn together provided that systematic modifications tailored to the needs of each individual child are put in place. Inclusive education is based on transforming the education system, unlike a special and integrated system of education, which primarily focus on changing the child to fit the system. Before the concept of IE and the 2006 UN Convention on the Rights of Persons with Disabilities, disability was predominately approached using the medical model. Now, however, the social model is widely employed in this field. Yet, the aim of "education for all" and IE is, for many countries, still in its infancy, including the countries of Central Asia, which already struggle to provide good education for all. For people with disabilities, especially children, all over the world, there is much work to be done to combat stigma and unfavorable attitudes, to adopt legal frameworks, adapt inclusive pedagogy, and ensure a proper infrastructure and transport systems and Tajikistan, the focus of this study, is no exception.

In this chapter, I aimed to show that there is still a long way to go to reach children in all parts of the country and to ensure that Tajik children with all kinds of disabilities have access to quality education that is tailored to their needs. Most state schools have no specially trained teaching staff, psychologists, social workers, therapists, or facilities and equipment to address the needs of children with disabilities. Children who need additional support are not entitled to an assistant to help them at school. Parents of children with disabilities often have to be very persistent to find their child a place in a state school, despite the fact that the right of disabled children to

---

[12] Interview with Sabohat Hakimzoda, Director of the Association of Parents of Children with Disabilities, Dushanbe, Zoom interview, 20 October 2021.

education is enshrined in national legislation, and even if they do, teachers are often unable or unwilling to tailor their teaching to the disabled child's needs. Children with disabilities and their parents still face a high level of stigmatization from other students, parents, and teachers. The general public tends to perceive disability as something to be pitied and disability issues are still approached using a medical model with very little evidence of a shift toward a social one.

References

Aiyubova Malohat N (2013) *Инклюзивное образование и его грани. Методическое пособие* [Inclusive Education and its Facets. A Toolkit]. Irfon, Dushanbe.
ASPBAE (Asia South Pacific Association for Basic and Adult Education) and Disabled Women's League 'Ishtirok' (2018) Analysis of the situation on inclusive education for people with disabilities in the Republic of Tajikistan. https://www.bit.ly/3oDyqLL
Bines H, Lei P (2011) Disability and education: the longest road to inclusion. Int J Educ Dev 31:419–424
Gevorgianiene V, Sumskiene E (2017) P.S. for post-Soviet: a glimpse to a life of persons with intellectual disabilities. J Intellect Disabil 21(3):235–247
Government of Tajikistan (GoT) (1994) Constitution of Tajikistan of 1994 with amendments through 2003. https://www.bit.ly/3oUHJHJ. Accessed 15 Oct 2021
Government of Tajikistan (GoT) (2010) Law of the Republic of Tajikistan on Social Protection of Persons with Disabilities of December 2010. (Approved by order of the government, # 675)
Government of Tajikistan (GoT) (2011) National Conceptual Framework for the Inclusive Education of CwD in Tajikistan for the period 2011–2015. (Approved by order of the government, # 288). https://www.bit.ly/2ZjKtmU
Government of Tajikistan (GoT) (2016) National Development Strategy of the Republic of Tajikistan for the period up to 2030. https://www.bit.ly/2TyLN2H
IPHR (2017) Tajikistan should mark the International Day of Persons with Disabilities by ratifying the Disability Rights Convention. Press release (1 December). https://www.bit.ly/3hjaeus
IPHR (2018) Persons with disabilities in Tajikistan: pushed to the margin (December). https://www.bit.ly/3BhgpFL
Jones H (2002) Disabled children's Rights, Enabling Education 6:8–9. https://www.bit.ly/3dpc7CQ
Muhammadieva B (2002) Children and disability in Tajikistan. State Committee for Statistics, Dushanbe, MONEE Country Analytical Report, May–June: 5–25.
Reiser R (2012) Implementing inclusive education: A commonwealth guide to implementing Article 24 of the UN CRPD (second edition). Commonwealth Secretariat, Marlborough House, Pall Mall, London
Save the Children (2016) Child protection situational analysis. Tajikistan 12. https://www.bit.ly/3oqoPHS
Save the Children (2020) The hardest places to be a child: Global Childhood Report 2020. https://www.bit.ly/3obHWnz
Stubbs S (2008) Inclusive education: Where there are few resources. Oslo, The Atlas Alliance. bit.ly/3hMtOz0
UN Commission on Human Rights (1990) Convention on the Rights of the Child. https://www.bit.ly/3TYGgwT
UN Committee on the Rights of the Child (2017) Concluding observations on the combined third to fifth periodic reports of Tajikistan. https://www.bit.ly/3jwmOqU

UN General Assembly (2006) Convention on the Rights of Persons with Disabilities: resolution/adopted by the General Assembly (24 January), A/RES/61/106. https://www.bit.ly/3lt GZHR

UN SDG General Assembly (2015) Transforming our world: the 2030 Agenda for Sustainable Development (21 October), A/RES/70/1. https://www.bit.ly/3yeVa76

UNESCO (1994) Salamanca statement on principles, policies and practice in Special Needs Education, World Conference on Special Needs Education: Access and Quality, Salamanca, Spain. https://www.bit.ly/3rNw1xZ

UNESCO (2008) Inclusive education: The way of the future. https://www.bit.ly/37cNztN

UNESCO (2017) A guide for ensuring inclusion and equity in education. https://www.bit.ly/3xgQIU3

UNESCO and GEM (2021) Central and Eastern Europe, Caucasus and Central Asia. Inclusion and education: All means all. https://www.bit.ly/3BeeP7K

UNICEF (2017) Inclusive Education—understanding Article 24 of the Convention on the Rights of Persons with Disabilities. https://www.uni.cf/3q5QrRW

UNICEF (2019) A quality and Inclusive Education for every child in Europe and Central Asia. https://www.uni.cf/3gs4zla

Wang HL (2009) Should all students with special educational needs (SEN) be included in mainstream education provision? Crit Analysis Int Educ Stud 2(4):154–161

Open Access This chapter is licensed under the terms of the Creative Commons Attribution 4.0 International License (http://creativecommons.org/licenses/by/4.0/), which permits use, sharing, adaptation, distribution and reproduction in any medium or format, as long as you give appropriate credit to the original author(s) and the source, provide a link to the Creative Commons license and indicate if changes were made.

The images or other third party material in this chapter are included in the chapter's Creative Commons license, unless indicated otherwise in a credit line to the material. If material is not included in the chapter's Creative Commons license and your intended use is not permitted by statutory regulation or exceeds the permitted use, you will need to obtain permission directly from the copyright holder.

Awareness in Central Asian States of Discrimination Against Labor Migrants

Kasiet Ysmanova

1 Introduction

According to the 1990 United Nations (UN) International Convention on the Protection of the Rights of All Migrant Workers and Members of their Families (ICRMW), the human rights of labor migrants should be given special attention. This has become part of the general awareness of, sensitivity to, and discussion on human rights in Central Asian societies.

According to World Bank data from 2018, remittances made up a total of 31% of Tajikistan's GDP. The corresponding figure for Kyrgyzstan was 33.3%, for Uzbekistan it was 9%, and for Kazakhstan 0.2% (Knomad and World Bank 2019). Despite the relatively low shares of remittances in the GDP of Uzbekistan and, notably, Kazakhstan, CAB Survey data[1] shows that remittances are equally important for respondents' financial circumstances in all five Central Asian states. Notably, the results were similar across all five countries, with approximately 70% of respondents reporting that remittances were important for their family's financial circumstances. This clearly shows not only the importance of remittances for the economies in the region but also illustrates that very large shares of Central Asian citizens are working as labor migrants abroad. Given these statistical indicators, it is worth investigating and initiating a critical discussion on the human rights situation of these migrants.

---

[1] The Central Asia Barometer Survey (CAB Survey) is a biannual large-scale research project that began in 2017. It measures the social, economic, and political atmosphere in Central Asian states, by conducting interviews with 1,000–2,000 respondents in each country. In the fall of 2021, the CAB Survey completed its tenth survey wave in Kazakhstan, Kyrgyzstan, Uzbekistan, Tajikistan, and Turkmenistan. Available at: https://ca-barometer.org/en/cab-database.

K. Ysmanova (✉)
Director/Researcher, Central Asia Barometer, Bishkek, Kyrgyzstan
e-mail: kasiet.ysmanova@ca-barometer.org

© The Author(s) 2023
A. Mihr and C. Wittke (eds.), *Human Rights Dissemination in Central Asia*, SpringerBriefs in Political Science,
https://doi.org/10.1007/978-3-031-27972-0_8

Russia is the host country for the majority of Central Asian (CA) labor migrants as substantial shares of the remittances to Central Asia come from Russia: 83% of Kyrgyzstan's, 58% of Tajikistan's, and 55% of Uzbekistan's in the first three quarters of 2021 according to the World Bank report (Ratha and Kim 2022). Another report, this time from the International Organization for Migration (IOM) states that about four million migrants from CA work in Russia: one million from Tajikistan, the same number from Kyrgyzstan, about two million from Uzbekistan, and 200,000 from Kazakhstan (IOM 2022).

It is a proven fact that labor migrants from CA face immense and numerous difficulties in Russia as well as some other countries, including exploitation by employers, low standards of living, unsafe and exhausting working conditions, and poor health services. As a result, they are at high risk of sustaining injuries and even dying due to poor working conditions, as is regularly reported by numerous news agencies and journalistic investigations covering labor migration in Russia (Redakciya 2021; Current Time 2021). According to Turaeva and Uriboyev, Central Asian labor migrants are often portrayed as "illegal", "illiterate", "wild", and "dangerous" in Russian public discourses and those with work permits still have trouble securing formal employment, leaving them open to abuse (Turaeva and Uriboyev 2021: 19–20).

There are also many concerns about the treatment of labor migrants in Turkey, which became the focus of public discussions in 2019 after the death of a Turkish MP's Uzbek housecleaner Nadira Kadirova (Eurasianet 2019). According to the Turkish ministry of the interior, Turkmenistan, Uzbekistan, and Kyrgyzstan are among the top ten countries whose citizens have permission to work in Turkey. In addition, in 2017, Uzbekistan also entered the top five countries in terms of the number of illegal migrants detained in Turkey (Russia Today 2019).

Public attitudes in all five CA countries concerning migration issues in general and the discrimination of compatriots working abroad is a topic that has received little attention from scholars conducting either scientific or applied research, in comparison to the breadth of research carried out on the public attitudes of hosting societies toward these migrants. Since 1989, the Levada Center has been regularly measuring xenophobia trends toward different groups within Russian society through its national surveys, which are part of the center's long-term studies focused on xenophobia, racism, and antisemitism. However, much less research has been conducted on the attitudes of the Russian public concerning the discrimination of labor migrants. A recent Levada study, using the Bogardus social distance scale, shows that the majority of the Russian population continues to maintain ethno-national and racial prejudices toward different groups, including labor migrants. Russians seem to be most distanced from the Roma and people from Africa, and Central Asia. In addition, over the past five years, the proportion of those who believe that the government should prevent the flow of migrants has grown from 58% to 68–73% (Levada Center 2022).

Much of the literature on the nexus of public opinion and discrimination toward labor migrants posits that the attitudes of a host society toward these migrants play an important role in shaping the policies, discriminatory or not, which impact them

(Tunon and Baruah 2012). Moreover, although, due to the varying levels of dependency on remittances, sending societies may be expected to have only weak leverage power to influence migration regimes in Russia and other host countries, the attitudes of the sending societies concerning such issues are in fact also important. It may seem that Central Asian migrants, on an individual level, are not in a position of power when negotiating with their job providers or with law enforcement officials. However, in Russia, Central Asian migrants are beginning to form different communities, some of which can be regarded as self-sufficient, based on various institutions including medical clinics, banks, cafes, schools, daycare facilities, and sophisticated money transfer services tailored to labor migrants (Ria Novosti 2013). Such efforts allow them to embrace some form of subjectivity and possibly enable them to develop collective action. In light of all this, discussions on Central Asian public opinion such as this one with a focus on issues of discrimination, have the potential to shed light on the effect that these attitudes have on the levels of discrimination faced by their labor migrants.

Moreover, the period between the fall of 2021 and the spring of 2022 saw many notable events, both on the regional and global levels. Russia's war against Ukraine is widely influencing Central Asian migration patterns. Asia-Plus reports that in the first quarter of 2022, more than 60,000 migrants returned to Tajikistan, which is 2.6 times more than last year (Asia-Plus 2022). Azizbek Yunusov, deputy head of the Agency for External Labor Migration of the Republic of Uzbekistan, recently stated that in the first quarter of the year, 133,000 labor migrants returned to Uzbekistan from Russia. Yunusov also shared data from a survey conducted among 150,000 citizens of Uzbekistan, in which 15% of those surveyed said that they had lost their jobs in Russia. Another 25% faced problems due to the unstable exchange rate and would therefore like to return to Uzbekistan (Migration Uzbekistan 2022). It is worth discussing how these events have influenced Central Asian public opinion on migration issues and the level of concern over the treatment of labor migrants abroad based on a comparison of the survey data from fall 2021 and spring 2022. It is also worth noting that, due to various factors, public opinion often fluctuates, and it is best to measure it weekly to be able to accurately monitor the trends. Nevertheless, comparing the results of two surveys conducted using similar methodology in different periods maybe also be useful.

2 Awareness of Migrant Rights in Five Central Asian Countries in Fall 2021 and Spring 2022

First, the study looked into the general awareness of human rights-related matters pertaining to migrants from all five Central Asian countries.[2] During the fall of 2021 and spring of 2022, in all five CA countries, Central Asia Barometer (CAB) asked a similar set of questions concerning migration also employing a similar methodology and simultaneously conducting fieldwork. This enabled a comparison of survey outcomes between countries. Within this study, simple random sampling (SRS) of mobile phone numbers was used to obtain a nationally representative sample (1,500 interviews per country) in Turkmenistan, Kazakhstan, Kyrgyzstan, Uzbekistan, and Tajikistan. In Kazakhstan, Kyrgyzstan, and Tajikistan, all interviews were conducted via desktop CATI[3] applications from either in-office or at-home stations. In Uzbekistan and Turkmenistan, all interviews were completed on tablets with calls made via mobile phones from at-home stations. Along with the migration section, questions were asked about media usage, the political and economic situation in each country, public health, attitudes toward the government, and opinions about other countries. In addition, questions aimed at gathering demographic information were included, such as age, education level, and employment status. The data is nationally representative in terms of gender, age group, and urban/rural divide. Assuming a simple random sample, with $p = 0.5$, at the 95% CI level, the margins of error (MOE) in all five countries are at 2.53%. Incorporating the mean design effects into these estimates yields margins of error of from 3.09% to 3.29% across countries (Central Asia Barometer 2022). In the following, we will discuss the main insights from these two surveys conducted across Central Asia before and after the war against Ukraine.

In general, the survey data suggests that the majority of respondents across Central Asia were concerned about how labor migrants from their countries were treated in other countries. When asked "How concerned are you, if at all, about the treatment of our country's labor migrants abroad?", around 55% (fall 2021) and 50% (spring 2021) of Uzbek respondents; 60% (fall 2021) and 62% (spring 2022) of Kazakh respondents; 85% (fall 2021) and 84% (spring 2022) of Kyrgyz respondents; 60% (fall 2021) and 70% (spring 2022) of Tajik respondents; 40% (fall 2021) and 57% (spring 2022) of Turkmen respondents answered they were very or somewhat concerned.

If we compare the fall and spring survey data, we can see that in Tajik and Turkmen societies there was a slight increase in concern about the issue, while this was not the case for other Central Asian countries. Consequently, we conclude that the topic of Russia's war against Ukraine and the consequent sanctions imposed on Russia had no notable influence on public opinion.

---

[2] This chapter examines the migration section of the fall 2021 wave and spring 2022 wave of the CAB Survey. The surveys, which included around 1,500 interviews per country, were conducted via telephone in Kazakhstan, Kyrgyzstan, Uzbekistan, Tajikistan, and Turkmenistan.

[3] CATI stands for computer-assisted telephone interviewing. With this method, telephone interviews are conducted using a questionnaire displayed on a computer screen. The interviewer records the responses using the keyboard and mouse to match the precoded responses displayed on the screen.

Pronounced divides in awareness

There appear to be significant differences in respondents' opinions on migration within urban and rural areas in Kazakhstan and Kyrgyzstan. Rural respondents showed a high level of concern, around 70% (very and somewhat concerned), about the treatment of their compatriots working abroad, while around 55% of urban dwellers gave this response. In Kyrgyzstan, rural respondents were just slightly more concerned about the topic. In the other countries of Central Asia, there were no significant differences in the opinions of urban and rural respondents. It can be inferred that, despite the fact that this did not apply to other Central Asian countries, communities in Kazakhstan and Kyrgyzstan are more informed about and aware of the issues faced by labor migrants abroad, which may, in turn, serve as an illustration of the urban/rural divide in migration patterns in these countries. Moreover, in Kyrgyzstan, urban respondents tended not to choose Russia as the most attractive country for labor migration. A total of 70% of rural respondents, in contrast to 55% of urban respondents, believe that Russia is the most attractive country.

In Kyrgyzstan, for example, there is a clear correlation between age and perception of Russia as the best country in which to work. The older the respondent is, the more attractive Russia appears to be for labor migration. Only approximately 55% of respondents aged between 18 and 29 years chose this option, compared to around 75% of those over the age of 60. However, this only applies to the Kyrgyz population and shows that the country's younger citizens are more actively exploring new destinations for labor migration, in contrast to the older generation.

In Kazakhstan, the level of concern about the treatment of labor migrants is clearly correlated with the age of the respondent—the higher the age, the greater the concern. However, in the case of the treatment of labor migrants abroad, only in Kazakhstan was there a significant difference in the level of concern. This may indicate that the younger generation is less informed about the issues these migrants face due to a lack of first-hand information or experience about the hardships of external labor migration. In other Central Asian countries, young people express similar levels of concern about the topic.

Another divide is along gender lines. In Tajikistan, when asked whether they had a family member who works in another country, around 70% of respondents answered in the affirmative. More female respondents reported having a family member abroad than male, with 75 and 55%, respectively. This may be due to the gendered differences in Tajik labor migration patterns, with numerous studies showing that Tajik external migration is male dominated.

When it comes to the questions regarding concern about the topic, there were no significant differences between genders, which may illustrate that women and men across all five nations are more or less equally informed on the topic.

Taking into account that most respondents in Tajikistan believe Russia is the most attractive country in which to work as a labor migrant and that a similar share of the population is concerned about the treatment of their labor migrants abroad, it can be concluded that respondents assess the "attractiveness" of the host country not based on their assumptions of good working conditions or societal acceptance, but based on the feasibility of securing work.

It seems that Tajik respondents see no other option for labor migration besides Russia with 90% reporting this to be the case. This high number could be due to several reasons including migration regimes. The same does not apply to other Central Asian countries, however, which, according to the survey data, have other country options at their disposal. For example, only 65% of Kyrgyz, 40% of Uzbek, 20% of Turkmen, and 15% of Kazakh respondents chose Russia. Tajikistan and Kazakhstan are at opposite ends of the spectrum here, with the vast majority of respondents in the former seeing Russia as the only option, and respondents in the latter being extremely divided on the issue, with only an insignificant share believing Russia to be the most suitable nation for its labor migrants.

Thus, the conclusion we come to is more counterintuitive. Despite all Central Asian countries being viewed as heavily dependent on remittances from Russia, this is largely only the case for Tajikistan and to a lesser degree for Kyrgyzstan. Central Asian populations are actively exploring other countries as destinations for labor migration starting with the nations closer to home, such as Kazakhstan and Turkey, as well as much more unexpected options, such as Canada, the USA, and Korea.

3 Discussion of the Survey Results in Light of Response and Nonresponse Bias in an Authoritarian Context

Each CA country showed a different level of concern about the treatment of their labor migrants abroad, both in fall 2021 and spring 2022, which could be due to a variety of reasons. Of course, the results should not be uniformly interpreted as implying that the less a sending population is concerned, the fewer issues their compatriots routinely experience in a host society. Clearly, there are differences between the Central Asian countries when it comes to migration patterns, destinations, and migration regimes in host countries, which to some extent may explain the differences in the levels of concern on the issue. There are, however, other factors and in the following, we will discuss the effect of the response and nonresponse bias within an authoritarian context, especially in Turkmenistan, Uzbekistan, and Tajikistan.

Response and nonresponse bias within the Central Asian context is one of the most pressing challenges for researchers in the region, due to the authoritarian nature of many of the political regimes and a general lack of awareness concerning survey research. Central Asian countries are some of the hardest in the world in which to conduct opinion polling and the CAB Survey faces various limitations: we cannot ask political, religious, or security-related questions, and before each survey, we need to obtain special permission from a governmental agency. Central Asia Barometer has experienced numerous incidents during fieldwork, such as interviewers being arrested and their survey tablets confiscated—even when they had formal permission letters at hand. Although there are no formal bans in place, these incidents have created a sense of insecurity among the research companies CAB works within these countries, increasing their self-censorship even further. This perceived and real risk of repressive action makes survey design and fieldwork a much longer, ambiguous, and difficult process, during which most political, economic, and religious questions are identified as sensitive. This applies to the different Central Asian countries to varying degrees, as CAB is freer to conduct survey research in Kazakhstan and Kyrgyzstan than in the other three countries.

In the following, we will discuss several "coping mechanisms" resulting from a fear of government sanctions, which respondents may use during interviews and which have a proven effect on response bias within an authoritarian context and as such should be taken into account when comparing the cross-country survey data on migration.

Respondents tend to choose the "don't know" answer option more frequently

Researchers usually do not read out the "don't know" answer option, thus omitting it from the questionnaire (Krosnick et al. 2002). This also applies to the CAB Survey. The reason for this approach is that respondents tend to choose this option more often, as it appears to be the safest and easiest when compared to other answer options. By choosing "don't know" respondents do not have to make an effort or risk their well-being. This is largely the case for other sections of the CAB Survey and, on average, Turkmen respondents tend to choose this option more than respondents from other Central Asian countries. For example, as the survey data shows, of all the CA countries, Turkmenistan seems to be the least concerned about the treatment of their labor migrants abroad. Yet, around 35% of Turkmen respondents chose the "don't know" option, while in other countries this answer option was generally selected by less than five percent of respondents, with the exception of Tajikistan. Consequently, the number of respondents who expressed their level of concern is lower than in the other countries surveyed. This is why when comparing countries we need to take into account that respondents in more closed countries such as Turkmenistan may choose the "don't know" option more frequently than others to avoid providing answers to certain questions which they believe would not be safe for their well-being.

Respondents refrain from expressing opinions that they think contradict their government's stance on a given issue

The question regarding concern about the treatment of labor migrants abroad attempts to shed light on negative manifestations of social life as it is related to the issues of discrimination and the government's inability to provide jobs at home. The Central Asian authorities face criticism over their inability to provide jobs and better protect their citizens in host countries, especially in Russia.

For example, in 2016, a total of 17 labor migrants working in Moscow died in a fire caused by poor working conditions and this tragic event has fueled public criticism of the Kyrgyz government (Current Time 2016). The fact that this question is related to the government's performance increases the risk of the results being skewed by a higher response bias and refusal bias (as a component of nonresponse bias).

Numerous studies have discussed the effect of the government's perceived position on respondents' answers. Chia (2014), for example, in her article for the *International Journal of Public Opinion Research* states that "in authoritarian countries, people's willingness to voice opinions may be a function of their perceptions of the government's stance, and individuals are likely to refrain from expressing opinions that appear to contradict the authority".

Respondents tend to try to provide answers that are identical to the perceived stance of the authorities on the given issue

In his recently published article, Marcus Tannenberg (2022) outlines the results of his multilevel analysis of surveys conducted in 37 African countries (with 228,000 respondents) to test for systematic bias. Tannenberg wanted to observe how respondents would answer certain questions when they believed that the government was conducting the survey, not independent researchers. This is also frequently the case in Central Asia. He concludes that the fear of sanctions from the government "induces a significant bias on questions regarding trust, approval and corruption perceptions in more autocratic countries, but not in more democratic countries" (591) and respondents tend to express more positive attitudes about issues raised in the questions asked. As outlined above, the question on the concern about labor migrants abroad is not only political but also directly related to the government's performance. Respondents in CA may answer that they are not concerned about the issue, because they perceive this to be the government's stance.

The systematic bias present in authoritarian contexts is a methodological concern that needs to be taken into account at all stages of survey research—especially when interpreting survey results concerning opinions related to the performance of the government. However, these tendencies do not mean that public opinion research is irrelevant in Central Asia or other authoritarian countries. According to Chang (1999) and his case study of public opinion in Singapore, even authoritarian authorities "have to concern themselves with managing perceived public opinion". In Central Asia, state media regularly highlights the popularity of the leader and the consensus among the people on the direction in which the country is moving and governmental policies in an attempt to influence not only individuals' opinions but also the people's perception of public opinion.

4 Conclusion

In sum, and as expected, due to the vast number of reports on discrimination against Central Asian labor migrants in Russia, respondents from Central Asian societies are mostly concerned about the treatment of their labor migrants abroad. In the CAB Survey, respondents in Central Asia expressed varying degrees of concern about this issue, which also needs to be analyzed in light of response and nonresponse bias in an authoritarian context, in addition to other factors.

References

Asia-Plus (2022) Skolko migrantov vernulos' iz Rossii za pervye tri mesyaca 2022 goda? https://asiaplustj.info/ru/news/tajikistan/society/20220408/skolko-migrantov-vernulos-iz-rossii-za-pervie-tri-mesyatsa-2022-goda. Accessed 10 July 2022

Central Asia Barometer (2022) Central Asia Barometer Survey data on migration. https://ca-barometer.org/en/publications. Accessed 10 July 2022

Chang T (1999) Reporting public opinion in Singapore. Harv Int J Press/polit 4:11–29

Chia S (2014) How Authoritarian social contexts inform individuals' opinion perception and expression. Int J Public Opin. Res. 26:384–396

Current Time (2016) "Esli by ona ne poehala, bedy by ne sluchilos'": Kyrgyzstan oplakivaet jenshin, pogibshih v Moskve". https://www.currenttime.tv/a/27952701.html. Accessed 10 July 2022

Current Time (2021) Kak obshestvo I SMI Rossii otnosyatsya k migrantam? Otvechaet professor Evropeyskogo universiteta Sergei Abashin. Current Time. https://www.currenttime.tv/a/russian-media-and-society-react-to-migrant-crisis-interview-/31602844.html. Accessed 30 June 2022

Eurasianet (2019) Death in Turkey shines light on Central Asian domestic workers. https://eurasianet.org/death-in-turkey-shines-light-on-central-asian-domestic-workers, https://blogs.worldbank.org/peoplemove/russia-ukraine-conflict-implications-remittance-flows-ukraine-and-central-asia, https://oxussociety.org/introducing-the-central-asia-migration-tracker/. Accessed 30 June 2022

International Migration Organization (2022) Sankcii protiv Rossii udarili po trudovym migrantam iz Centralnoi Azii. https://news.un.org/ru/story/2022/06/1425932. Accessed 30 June 2022

Knomad and World Bank Group (2019) Migration and Development Brief 31. Knomad. https://www.knomad.org/publication/migration-and-development-brief-31. Accessed 30 June 2022

Krosnick JA, Holbrook AL et al (2002) The impact of "no opinion" response options on data quality. Non-attitude reduction or an invitation to satisfy? Public Opin Q 66:371–403

Levada Center (2022) Ksenofobiya i Migranty. Levada Center. https://www.levada.ru/2022/01/24/ksenofobiya-i-migranty/. Accessed 30 June 2022

Migration Uzbekistan (2022) Agentlik Hakida. http://www.migration.uz/post/view/80. Accessed 10 July 2022

Ratha and Kim (2022) Russia-Ukraine Conflict: Implications for Remittance flows to Ukraine and Central Asia. https://blogs.worldbank.org/peoplemove/russia-ukraine-conflict-implications-remittance-flows-ukraine-and-central-asia. Accessed 30 June 2022

Redakciya (2021) Skrytaya Jizn' Trudovyh Migrantov v Rossii. Redakciya. https://www.youtube.com/watch?v=yq-JlJGv8Dk. Accessed 30 June 2022

Ria Novosti (2013) Tadjikski rep, kirgizski klub. Nochnaya jizn' gastarbayterov. https://ria.ru/20131127/979852536.html?in=t. Accessed 10 July 2022

Russia Today (2019) Diplomat: dlya migrantov iz Azii Turciya stala privlekatelnee Rossii. Russia Today. https://russian.rt.com/inotv/2019-01-12/Diplomat-dlya-migrantov-iz-Azii. Accessed 30 June 2022

Tannenberg M (2022) The autocratic self-bias: censorship of regime support. Democratization 4:591–610

Tunon M, Baruah N (2012) Public attitudes towards migrant workers in Asia. Migr Dev (1)1:149–162

Turaeva R, Uriboyev R (2021) Labour, mobility and informal practices in Russia, Central Asia, and Eastern Europe. Routledge, London and New York

Open Access This chapter is licensed under the terms of the Creative Commons Attribution 4.0 International License (http://creativecommons.org/licenses/by/4.0/), which permits use, sharing, adaptation, distribution and reproduction in any medium or format, as long as you give appropriate credit to the original author(s) and the source, provide a link to the Creative Commons license and indicate if changes were made.

The images or other third party material in this chapter are included in the chapter's Creative Commons license, unless indicated otherwise in a credit line to the material. If material is not included in the chapter's Creative Commons license and your intended use is not permitted by statutory regulation or exceeds the permitted use, you will need to obtain permission directly from the copyright holder.

Gender Equality and International Human Rights Law in Kyrgyzstan

Aizhan Erisheva

1 Introduction

Gender inequality is one of the main issues in Central Asia due to the inherited patriarchal culture, the low prioritization of the problem at the country level, and poor representation of women in decision-making processes. In the case of Kyrgyzstan, in the last couple of years, the news headlines have been filled with sad stories of women suffering from domestic and gender-based violence and discrimination. It appears that women's rights and interests are not protected, not monitored, and not considered as a part of the state's agenda. The surprising element is that Kyrgyzstan was the pioneer in the region when it came to adopting laws that promote human rights. Kyrgyzstan ratified the following international human rights treaties to protect women's rights: the International Covenant on Economic, Social and Cultural Rights (ICESCR) in 1994 (UN 1966b), the International Covenant on Civil and Political Rights (ICCPR) in 1994 (UN 1966a), the Convention on the Elimination of All Forms of Discrimination against Women (CEDAW) in 1997 (UN 1979), the International Convention on the Elimination of All Forms of Racial Discrimination (CERD) in 1997 (UN 1966c), the Forced Labour Convention (ILO 1930) and Equal Remuneration Convention (ILO 1951), both ratified in 1992, the Abolition of Forced Labour Convention in 1999 (ILO 1957), the Discrimination (Employment and Occupation) Convention (ILO 1958) and the Employment Policy Convention (ILO 1964), both ratified in 1992, and many other human rights treaties.

In addition to the ratification of international human rights instruments and cooperation with international human rights structures, the Kyrgyz government has made commitments regarding the achievement of the Sustainable Development Goals (SDGs) (National Statistical Committee 2020), especially SDG 5, which aims to

---

A. Erisheva (✉)
Monitoring and Evaluation Researcher, Bishkek, Kyrgyzstan
e-mail: a.erisheva@osce-academy.net

"achieve gender equality and empower all women and girls", but also the rest of the SDGs, since gender-related issues are intersectional, and each SDG includes a gender component (Sustainable Development Report 2021).

Since the referendum on 5 May 2021, the Constitution of the Kyrgyz Republic states: "No one may be discriminated against based on sex, race, language, disability, ethnicity, religion, age, political or any other opinion, education, origin, property or any other status, or other circumstances" (Sect. 2, Chap. Human Rights in Central Asia—Between Internationalization and Nation-Building, Article 24.1) and "In the Kyrgyz Republic, men and women have equal rights and freedoms and equal opportunities for their implementation" (Sect. 2, Chap. Human Rights in Central Asia—Between Internationalization and Nation-Building, Article 24.3). Moreover, Sect. 2 of the Constitution sets out Personal Rights and Freedoms (Chap. Human Rights in Central Asia: Challenges and Perspectives, Articles 25–36), Political Rights (Chap. Human Rights Education and Human Rights in Central Asia, Articles 37–39), Economic and Social Rights (Chap. Human Rights as a Concept of Public Law: Challenges for Central Asian Higher Education Systems, Articles 40–50), Rights and Responsibilities of Citizens (Chap. Transnational Higher Education—The Case of Kazakhstan, Articles 41–54), and Guarantees of Human and Civil Rights and Freedoms (Chap. Redesigning the Law Curriculum in Uzbekistan, Articles 55–65) (Constitution of the Kyrgyz Republic 2021). Hence, the Law of the Kyrgyz Republic On State Guarantees of Equal Rights and Equal Opportunities for Men and Women (of 4 August 2008, No. 184) ensures gender equality and the effective implementation of the constitutional norms, but largely fails to do so in practice (Law on Equal Rights and Opportunities 2008). Irrespective of these recent changes in the constitution, the government's first long-term National Gender Strategy (NGS) on Achieving Gender Equality by (2020) was adopted in 2012 in compliance with CEDAW (Asian Development Bank 2019; National Strategy on Gender Equality 2015), and a National Action Plan for 2022–2024 was developed and implemented. Furthermore, it launched a long-term National Development Strategy until 2040 (National Development Strategy 2018) and is currently updating the National Strategy for Achieving Gender Equality until 2030. In addition, the government ratified more than 50 international covenants and has a strong legal base to protect women's rights. Despite all this, however, violence and discrimination against women and girls remain high (International Alert 2021; UN Women 2020, 2022; CEDAW 2022).

2 Gender-Related Socioeconomic Rights in Kyrgyzstan

Kyrgyzstan is a lower-middle-income country with a GDP per capita of 1,276 US Dollars in 2021 (World Bank 2021). The country's economy heavily depends on the mining sector (mostly gold production), remittances, and resale. Kyrgyzstan is ranked fourth among those economies whose GDP depends on remittances. According to the data for 2021, the share of remittances in GDP was 33% (Migration Data Portal 2022a, b). The total number of emigrants reached 774,400 people by 2020, and more than half of them (59.6%) were women (ibid.). The main destination countries are Russia, Kazakhstan, Turkey, and South Korea, where migrant women are mostly employed in the service sector, retail, catering, cleaning, beauty services, domestic work, and textile sector. One of the main reasons for the feminization of migration is the socioeconomic situation in the country and the existing gender inequality in the labor market.

In 2020, the male labor force participation rate was 74.4%, while the female labor force participation rate was 46.1%, illustrating that women are less represented in the local labor market. Women work predominantly in so-called female-dominated sectors, such as education (78.8% women), public health and social security (78.2% women), and in real estate (95.8% women). One of the main reasons for women's low participation in the labor market is the inherited patriarchal culture and associated gender stereotypes and discrimination (National Statistical Committee 2021).

Within the family, the roles of men and women tend to be strictly divided, with the man as the breadwinner and the woman as the keeper of the hearth. Once they are married, most women are not willing, nor do they have an opportunity to pursue a career because they would have to balance work and household chores (Kleinbach & Salimjanova 2007, 217–233; Ibraeva et al. 2011). According to a time-use survey, household work in Kyrgyzstan is largely considered a woman's responsibility, since women devoted an average of 4 h 33 min a day to household chores, spending 18.1% of their time on them; while men spent less than an hour (55 min) per day on household chores, which corresponds to approximately 3.9% of their daily time budget. As a result, compared to men, women spend almost five times more time on housework and 2.3 times more time on raising children (Kleinbach & Salimjanova 2007, 245–55). Therefore, when making a career choice, women sought out those occupations where they can combine their primary job outside the home with a "second shift" (Hochschildand Machung 2012) at home (UNECE 2021; UN Women Kyrgyzstan Country Office 2018a; Kolpashnikova and Kan 2020).

In Kyrgyzstan, much like the other countries in Central Asia, gender stereotypes also influence the upbringing and education of girls. According to the Global Gender Gap Index (GGGI), Kyrgyzstan received 0.996 for educational attainment (literacy rate of 0.998, enrollment in primary education 0.993, enrollment in secondary education 1, enrollment in tertiary education 1) in 2022 (WEF 2022). This indicates that women and girls have equal access to education, and the number of women with higher education exceeds that of men. The problem, however, is the prevailing stereotypes regarding the traditionally female and traditionally male degree subjects.

These stereotypes remain in children's and people's minds from when adults give dolls and tea sets to girls and cars and toy tools to boys. These seemingly harmless actions affected the women's and men's choices regarding their future professions. The census shows that in the academic year 2020–2021, the top three areas selected by female students were education (about 86% of the total number of students), humanities (more than 73%), service provision (more than 63%), while male students mainly chose professions related to architecture and construction (about 82%), agriculture (about 75%), technical sciences (over 69%) (Kleinbach and Salimjanova 2007, 144–60).

Not only do women participate less in the labor market, but they are also paid less than men. Thus, according to the data, the average monthly salary of men was 19,992 Kyrgystani som in 2020,[1] while the average monthly salary of women in 2020 did not even reach men's 2016 level (15,592 Kyrgystani som[2]) and in fact only earned a monthly average of 15,072 Kyrgystani som.[3] Women were not only paid less than men but also worked in all the lowest paid sectors (listed above), while men mostly worked in the higher paid sectors, such as finance and insurance (61.9% of employees in this sector are men), information and communication (59.2%), and mining (95.6%) (Kleinbach and Salimjanova 2007, 80–103).

The main reason for the disparity between women's and men's wage levels is occupational segregation. As mentioned above, women were mostly employed in lower-paid sectors, especially in Kyrgyzstan, where salaries for education, healthcare, and social security sectors are based on the state budget and are far from market levels. However, the sector factor is not the only reason for the gender pay gap because even within one sector, men and women usually do not earn the same (UN Women 2018; Ribeiro 2011; Akbulaev and Aliyeva 2020; Urbaeva et al. 2019).

Let's compare women and men with the same level of education working in the same sector. Women always have less experience and fewer opportunities for career growth due to the time spent on child-rearing, which as a result, affects women's earnings. If we look at the employment of women and men disaggregated by age group, we can see that, in general, the employment level of men is higher than women in all age groups. However, the gap within the 25–34 year age group is the highest at about 40%. This is the age at which women tend to leave their jobs to have children (Kleinbach and Salimjanova 2007, 217–33).

The last reason behind wage differences is stereotypes and discrimination. According to the conservative gender norms in Kyrgyz society, women are mostly portrayed as mothers and wives rather than experts in any field. Although they contribute to the family budget, work with their husbands, and sometimes alone, women still face and indeed accept the societal belief that their primary role is at home, raising children, and doing household work (Kolpashnikova and Kan 2020). These stereotypes mostly lead to employers perceiving women as higher risk than men because they often unexpectedly leave their jobs to get married or have children, even if they stay, they are less dedicated and hardworking. Thus, employers discriminate against women when recruiting and setting wage levels as they feel they need to compensate for the abovementioned costs by proposing lower wages.

According to the Women and Migration Study and Gender in Society Perception Study conducted by the UN Women Country Office in Bishkek, women emigrated not only with their male partners or relatives but also independently to improve the

---

[1] Approximately equal to 240.15 US dollars, calculated according to the exchange rate of the National Bank as of 29 October 2022. URL: https://www.nbkr.kg/getservice.jsp?lang=ENG.

[2] Approximately equal to 187.30 US dollars, calculated according to the exchange rate of the National Bank as of 29 October 2022. URL: https://www.nbkr.kg/getservice.jsp?lang=ENG.

[3] Approximately equal to 181.05 US dollars, calculated according to the exchange rate of the National Bank as of 29 October 2022. URL: https://www.nbkr.kg/getservice.jsp?lang=ENG.

financial welfare of their families. The main destinations for women emigrating from Kyrgyzstan were Russia, the Arabian Peninsula, and Europe. Moreover, the study revealed a new cohort of migrant women who are younger, more educated, mostly from urban areas, and have higher socioeconomic status. These women primarily emigrated for personal reasons. Women emigrate for personal reasons, mostly to avoid the local constraints frustrating their goals. Some emigrate for new professional, social, and personal opportunities, but personal reasons are often related to security concerns (UN Women 2019).

Personal and human security is another reason women emigrate. The issues include a range from physical and verbal abuse to health and economic security. The reasons women suffer at home and are driven to try to escape this situation can vary from family to family. However, the roots of the problem remain patriarchal norms and traditions. While married women mostly tried to escape from domestic violence, abusive relationships, psychological abuse from husbands and in-laws, unmarried women usually tried to escape from family pressure, arranged marriages, and harmful practices or so-called bride kidnapping. These patriarchal norms have taken root in our society and thus affected every woman regardless of her age, marital status, education, or background (ibid.).

However, emigration is not only a chance for women to escape from the physical and psychological violence or an opportunity for emancipation. It can also lead to economic violence. According to the Alternative Report on the Implementation of CEDAW, daughters are more industrious and forbearing and are more willing to sacrifice their interests for the good of the family. Consequently, women are seen as the more attractive target for emigration. Many young unmarried women (approximately 60%, according to the International Organization for Migration, IOM) emigrate to another country because of parental debt. Their parents send them out to work or allow them to leave to earn money to save the family from poverty (UN CEDAW et al. 2019). Many women spent all their time, wasted their youth, and sacrificed their health and their careers to earn money and send remittances home. The women themselves usually do not even have access to the money they earn, since their parents, in-laws, and husbands decide how the money is to be allocated. They are asked to organize and pay for celebratory events, buy toys for the family's children, build houses, finish renovations, and at the end of the day, still have no access to savings or any savings.

There is a plethora of case studies and stories about a woman being abused in many ways by their families. In Jala-Abad, a major city in central Kyrgyzstan, one woman returned home, having worked three years as a labor migrant in Russia, to find that her money had been used to renovate her father-in-law's house and buy ten bulls to add to the family's herd. She spent another year tending the house and the bulls, dreaming that when the cattle were sold, she and her husband would be able to invest in their daughter's education. But after a year her husband decided to fulfill his obligation as a good Muslim son, sending his parents on a Muslim pilgrimage or "haj" to Saudi Arabia, using the money received from selling the bulls instead of investing it into his daughter's education (IOM 2018).

3 Domestic and Gender-Based Violence

Domestic violence is one of the most challenging issues in Kyrgyzstan because women are a priori believed to be guilty with no opportunity to defend themselves. Even parents, children, and close relatives do not support women subjected to domestic violence, tending more to criticize them. During the 2020 lockdown and quarantine, all preexisting gender issues were exacerbated. The closure of social facilities and the spread of the virus led to a rise in unpaid domestic work. The reason for this was not only a lack of sufficient support or less protection from exploitation but also the aforementioned traditional norms and stereotypes which burden women with all care and domestic work.

The COVID-19 pandemic deepened the global recession and political developments resulted in an economic downturn that has further distanced women from access to opportunities and resources, making them fully financially dependent on male family members. This financial dependency, combined with the physical inability to escape, get help, and access justice, put women at risk of becoming victims of domestic violence, and the increase in reported cases supports this assumption. For instance, from the introduction of the state of emergency, the registered domestic violence cases were 65% higher than in the same period in 2019. The reported cases included physical, psychological, economic, and sexual violence and neglect; and 95% of victims were women in the 21–50 year age range (UN Women 2020).

However, this is the tip of the iceberg because it is assumed that most victims do not report their abuse to the police. The National Statistical Committee (NSC) estimates that, in 2020, the number of people convicted and sentenced for misdemeanors related to domestic violence following the code of the Kyrgyz Republics on misdeeds was only 290 (about 87% of whom were men). Many of the cases (approximately 76%) were related to domestic violence (Art. 75), about 21% were for inflicting minor injury (Art. 66), beating (Art. 65) less than 1%, and disorderly conduct (Art. 119) about 2%. In that same year, over 9,600 people applied to crisis centers and other specialized institutions providing socio-psychological assistance to the population due to domestic violence. Most of these (86%) were women (Kleinbach and Salimjanova 2007, 223–44).

According to the statistics provided by the NSC, only 798 women were treated for injuries resulting from violence in the family in 2020. If we look at the cases by types of violence, about 97% were treated as a result of physical violence, about 1% as a result of psychological violence, and about 2% as a result of sexual violence. When it comes to the use of forensic expertise, only 180 women requested a forensic examination, about 88% were cases of physical violence, 10% were cases of psychological violence, and only about 2% due to sexual violence (ibid.). From the statistics provided above it is clear that the majority of the cases are still hidden and only a small fraction of the victims of violence reported their abusers, tried to get a forensic examination, or treatment at a hospital (ibid.).

3.1 Gender Bias in the Legal System and Cultural Norms

One of the main factors behind this problem is an ineffective legal system with legal loopholes that put female victims of domestic violence at risk because any protection orders that are issued are mostly not enforced and monitored. According to the article on domestic violence of the Code of Misdemeanors of the Kyrgyz Republic (Art. 70), there are only two types of punishment: 48 h of community service or arrest and being held in custody for a period of three to seven days. At first sight this may seem like a very effective system, which is not punitive and more focused on the correction. However, it demotivates female victims of violence from reporting abuse as they fear reprisal (Code of Misdemeanors 2021).

Another factor is the cultural norms and stereotypes that mean domestic violence is tolerated. Reporting domestic violence is mostly seen in a negative light, with society blaming the victim in the belief that women should keep the incidents behind closed doors. There are many cases of women withdrawing their complaints under pressure from parents, in-laws, relatives, and society. And as we can see from the data above, women mostly report physical violence, while psychological and sexual violence tends to be considered taboo or as less important. However, in most cases, physical violence goes hand in hand with sexual violence and nearly always psychological abuse (Childress 2017; Childress et al. 2017).

There is a common perception that women cannot be raped by their husbands. Forced sexual activity after bride kidnapping should be classified as rape but people use psychological pressure to try to legitimize the sexual violence through the *"nikah"* (marriage contract), parents' approval, and the oft-heard *"el emne deyt"* (what people will say) to portray public expectations. According to the study by the United Nations Population Fund (UNFPA) and the NSC, "more than half of all respondents believe that kidnapped women who were forced to engage in sex with their kidnappers must report being raped to law enforcing bodies. However, only 30% of them expressed willingness to actually accept their own female relatives in such a situation back home. Sadly, a considerable percentage, 25% of women and nearly 30% of men, believe that victims of kidnapping must marry their rapists. This answer is twice as widespread among rural population" (UN Women 2018b).

4 Sexual Reproductive Health and Human Rights

Sexual and reproductive health (SRH) is one of the least discussed topics in Kyrgyzstan. Stereotypes and prejudice related to the issue prevail and the majority of the population are not fully aware about SRH and preventive measures. In 2020, the average age at first marriage was 23.4 years for women and 27.2 years for men. Compared to 2016 year, the age of marriage for women decreased by 0.2 years, while for men, in contrast, it increased by 0.1 years (Kleinbach and Salimjanova 2007, 61). Women usually only have their first sexual health consultation with gynecologists after they are married or even only during pregnancy, a problem that especially applies to women from rural areas.

One of the factors influencing such attitudes and behavior is the lack of specialists in remote regions (especially when it comes to health workers specialized in adolescent health). With the majority of hospitals and family medical centers located in the *rayon* (district) capitals, due to the distance, time spent, and costs associated with visits women mostly refuse to visit hospital. However, the affordability and accessibility of medical consultations are not the only reasons. There is also a "cult of virginity" that influences women's decision-making regarding whether to attend a consultation, since there is a strong perception that unmarried women must be virgin or "pure" and there is therefore no need for a medical examination.

When it comes to family planning, almost 77% of women believed that they should have the final say in decisions regarding their own health, and 76.6% of women of reproductive age reported that they made their own SRH decisions (WHO 2021). However, in 2020, only 16.6% of women of reproductive age (WRA) used contraceptives (Kleinbach and Salimjanova 2007, 166). The most popular methods of contraception were intrauterine devices (IUDs) (52.6%), male condoms (34.9%), and the pill (7.7%) (ibid.). The popularity of IUDs can be explained by the financial factor since women can get this form of contraception for free. In contrast, the free distribution of male condoms was stopped due to a lack of funds from development organizations over the last couple of years. However, in addition to the financial factor, there is the perception among men that family planning and contraception are primarily the woman's responsibility.

In contrast, the man should enjoy the process, and nothing should distract or restrict him, even condoms. Thus, according to the Multiple Indicator Cluster Survey (MICS) conducted by the United Nations Children's Fund (UNICEF) in the Kyrgyz Republic, "the male condom turned out to be not the most popular method of protection—only 10.4% of men are prepared to 'spoil the pleasure.' But 22.4% of women are prepared to put in an intrauterine device to avoid unwanted pregnancy" (Skolisheva 2015; NSC et al. 2016).

A total of 99.3% of births are attended by medical professionals (Kleinbach and Salimjanova 2007, 217–233). Almost all women receive antenatally. 99.8% attended the antenatal clinic at least once, and 94.3% attended at least four times and postnatal checkups. 96.1% received a postnatal checkup within the first two days of giving birth (Kleinbach and Salimjanova 2007, 166). Based on these results, it can be inferred that women are well-treated and that the population has a high awareness about pregnancy and childbirth. The perception that women are responsible for the sexual education and health of the child prevails in Kyrgyz communities. In addition, if women do not give birth to a boy, they are considered unsuccessful as a woman and wife and as failing in their primary duty of giving birth to an heir.

Most SRH issues could be addressed or prevented, however, cultural norms and stereotypes in Kyrgyz society mean this does not happen. Combined with a lack of knowledge about health issues and access to reliable information, this results in women often only consulting a medical professional once they have recovered or at the final stages of their illness. At the same time, in some cases, the lack of sexual education led to discrimination and stigmatization.

5 Conclusion

Since independence, Kyrgyzstan has had a good track record in implementing international human rights treaties that promote and protect women's rights. The government has ratified more than 50 international human rights treaties, cooperated with international bodies, and adopted domestic legislation to comply with international standards. However, the de facto situation regarding the women's rights is quite challenging. Women of all ages and from different socioeconomic backgrounds still face discrimination in all spheres of life. The commitments to promote and protect women's economic rights under the ICESCR and CEDAW that have not been fulfilled include an agreement to provide: "full and productive employment under conditions safeguarding fundamental political and economic freedoms to the individual" (Part III, Art. 6.), to "pair wages and equal remuneration for work of equal value without distinction of any kind, in particular women being guaranteed conditions of work not inferior to those enjoyed by men, with equal pay for equal work" (Part III, Art.7), to provide social protection with an agreement that "special protection should be accorded to mothers during a reasonable period before and after childbirth. During such period, working mothers should be accorded paid leave or leave with adequate social security benefits" (Part III, Art. 10.2) (UN 1966b). As a result, the reality is a low employment rate of women, poor working conditions without labor and social protection, a gender pay gap, a lack of maternity protection, and unequal division of household work (World Bank 2021).

Increased gender-based and domestic violence due to the "weak enforcement and monitoring of the implementation of the Act on Protection and Defense against Domestic Violence", failure to criminalize certain types of violence such as marital rape, "impunity for perpetrators, the limited enforcement of protection orders, the lack of victim support and the barriers to women's and girls' access to justice in cases of gender-based violence, including revictimization during criminal proceedings" (ibid.). Hence, limited access to sexual and reproductive health and rights there is a "low rate of condom use, high abortion rates among adolescent women", and overall "persistence of patriarchal attitudes and discriminatory stereotypes concerning the roles and responsibilities of women and men in the family and in society, exacerbated by growing religious influence, and the lack of a comprehensive strategy to address such gender stereotypes" (ibid.).

There are several factors that have led to this situation. First, the country has an inherited patriarchal culture and norms that result in gender stereotypes, prejudice, and discrimination. Second, the country's socioeconomic situation limits the rights of women and creates obstacles such as a lack of knowledge, lack of education, and lack of information.

The third aspect is that most of the international human rights treaties were ratified by the government as a part of the terms and conditions to receive grants, soft loans, or preferential status (such as through the EU's generalized scheme of preferences, GSP +). Therefore, donors need to review and reconsider their monitoring procedures for women's health in Kyrgyzstan. When it comes to holding the government to account, the focus must not only be on the ratification of the treaties but also the enforceability of the law as well as the legislative framework, its "legally undefined terms of morality, ethics and traditional family values in the context of the ongoing large-scale inventory of legislation, which can be used to undermine women's rights" (ibid.). Nowadays, a lot of work is being done by the development sector. However, the campaigns/programs should be conducted at the country level and should be focused not on resolving the issues but more on tackling the roots of the problems and preventing them from arising in the first place. Increasing access to education, information, and resources to reduce women's financial dependency and providing science and fact-based gender-related messages and education through social media.

References

ADC Memorial and Kyrgyz Family Planning Alliance (2019) Alternative information on Kyrgyzstan's implementation of the UN CEDAW in connection with the review of the state report by the UN CEDAW (November). https://adcmemorial.org/wp-content/uploads/kyrgyzstan-loi-cedaw-76-pswg-sept-2019-adc-memorial-kaps-en.doc.pdf. Accessed 3 Oct 2022

Akbulaev N, Aliyeva B (2020) Gender and economic growth: Is there a correlation? The example of Kyrgyzstan. Cogent Econ Financ 8(1), 1758007. https://www.academia.edu/81827658/Gender_and_economic_growth_Is_there_a_correlation_The_example_of_Kyrgyzstan?sm=b. Accessed 13 Nov 2022

Asian Development Bank, Kyrgyz Republic (2019) Country Gender Assessment (December). https://www.adb.org/sites/default/files/institutional-document/546966/kyrgyz-republic-country-gender-assessment-2019.pdf. Accessed 30 Oct 2022

Childress S, Gioia D, Campbell JC (2017) Women's strategies for coping with the impacts of domestic violence in Kyrgyzstan: a grounded theory study. Social Work in Health Care. https://doi.org/10.1080/00981389.2017.1412379. Accessed November 12, 2022

Childress S (2017) "Plates and Dishes Smash; Married Couples Clash": Cultural and Social Barriers to Help-Seeking Among Women Domestic Violence Survivors in Kyrgyzstan. Violence Against Women 1–23. https://www.academia.edu/81729065/_Plates_and_Dishes_Smash_Married_Couples_Clash_Cultural_and_Social_Barriers_to_Help_Seeking_Among_Women_Domestic_Violence_Survivors_in_Kyrgyzstan?sm=b. Accessed 14 Nov 2022

Code of Misdemeanors of the Kyrgyz Republic, dated 28 October 2021, No.128, Centralized Database of Legal Information of the Kyrgyz Republic. http://cbd.minjust.gov.kg/act/view/ru-ru/112306. Accessed 12 Nov 2022

Committee on the Elimination of Discrimination against Women (2022) CEDAW Concluding observations on the fifth periodic report of Kyrgyzstan. https://documents-dds-ny.un.org/doc/UNDOC/GEN/N21/351/71/PDF/N2135171.pdf?OpenElement. Accessed 12 Nov 2022

Constitution of the Kyrgyz Republic, enacted by the Law of the Kyrgyz Republic (2021) Centralized Database of Legal Information of the Kyrgyz Republic. http://cbd.minjust.gov.kg/act/view/ru-ru/112213?cl=ru-ru. Accessed 30 Oct 2022

Hochschild A, Machung A (2012) The second shift: Working parents and the revolution at home. London, Penguin. https://books.google.kg/books?id=St_6kWcPJS8C&pg=PT3&source=gbs_selected_pages&cad=2#v=onepage&q&f=false. Accessed 12 Nov 2022

Ibraeva G, Moldosheva F, Niyazova A (2011) Kyrgyz Country Case Study. Background paper for the World Development Report 2012: Gender Equality and Development. Washington D.C., World Bank. https://openknowledge.worldbank.org/bitstream/handle/10986/9151/WDR2012-0025.pdf?sequence=1&isAllowed=y. Accessed 12 Nov 2022

International Alert (2021) How we challenged the 65% rise in domestic violence in Kyrgyzstan, June 2021. https://www.international-alert.org/stories/how-we-challenged-65-rise-domestic-violence-kyrgyzstan/. Accessed 12 Nov 2022

International Labour Organization (ILO) (1930) Forced Labour Convention, No. 29, Information System on International Labour Standards. https://www.ilo.org/dyn/normlex/en/f?p=1000:12100:0::NO::P12100_ILO_CODE:C029. Accessed 12 Nov 2022

International Labour Organization (ILO) (1951) Equal Remuneration Convention, No. 100, Information System on International Labour Standards. https://www.ilo.org/dyn/normlex/en/f?p=NORMLEXPUB:12100:0::NO::P12100_Ilo_Code:C100. Accessed 12 Nov 2022

International Labour Organization (ILO) (1958) Discrimination (Employment and Occupation) Convention, No. 111, Information System on International Labour Standards. https://www.ilo.org/dyn/normlex/en/f?p=NORMLEXPUB:12100:0::NO::P12100_Ilo_Code:C111. Accessed 12 Nov 2022

International Labour Organization (ILO) (1964) Employment Policy Convention, No. 122, Information System on International Labour Standards. https://www.ilo.org/dyn/normlex/en/f?p=NORMLEXPUB:55:0::NO::P55_TYPE,P55_LANG,P55_DOCUMENT,P55_NODE:CON,en,C122,/Document#:~:text=1.,productive%20and%20freely%20chosen%20employment. 12 Novr 2022

International Labour Organization (1957) Abolition of Forced Labour Convention (No. 105). Information System on International Labour Standards, International Labour Organization. https://www.ilo.org/dyn/normlex/en/f?p=NORMLEXPUB:12100:0::NO::P12100_ILO_CODE:C105. Accessed 12 Nov 2022

International Organization for Migration (IOM) (2018) The Fragile Power of Migration: The needs and rights of women and girls from Tajikistan and Kyrgyzstan who are affected by migration. Sub-Regional Office for Central Asia.. https://kazakhstan.iom.int/sites/g/files/tmzbdl1586/files/documents/02.pdf. Accessed 7 Oct 2022

Kleinbach R, Salimjanova L (2007) Kyz ala kachuu and adat: non-consensual bride kidnapping and tradition in Kyrgyzstan. Central Asian Surv 26: 217–233. https://www.researchgate.net/publication/240523975_Kyz_ala_kachuu_and_adat_non-consensual_bride_kidnapping_and_tradition_in_Kyrgyzstan. Accessed 13 Nov 2022

Kolpashnikova K, Kan M-Y (2020) Gender Gap in Housework: Couples' Data Analysis in Kyrgyzstan. J Comp Fam Stud 51(2):154–187. https://www.jstor.org/stable/26976642. Accessed 12 Nov 2022

Law of the Kyrgyz Republic On State Guarantees of Equal Rights and Equal Opportunities for Men and Women, dated 4 August 2008, No. 184. Centralized Database of Legal Information of the Kyrgyz Republic. http://cbd.minjust.gov.kg/act/view/ru-ru/202398. Accessed 30 Oct 2022

Migration Data Portal (2022) Key trends. https://www.migrationdataportal.org/themes/remittances#:~:text=In%202021%2C%20the%20top%20five,billion)%20. Accessed 25 Oct 2022

Migration Data Portal (2022) Migration Statistics. https://www.migrationdataportal.org/international-data?i=stock_abs_&t=2020&cm49=417. Accessed 25 Oct 2022

National Development Strategy of the Kyrgyz Republic for 2018–2040, Government Programmes. https://www.gov.kg/ru/programs/8. Accessed 13 Nov 2022

National Statistical Committee, UNICEF, UNFPA (2016) Multiple Indicator Cluster Survey, Final Report. https://www.unicef.org/kyrgyzstan/media/1066/file/Kyrgyzstan_2014_MICS_English.pdf%20.pdf. Accessed 14 Nov 2022

National Statistical Committee of the Kyrgyz Republic (2020) Monitoring of Sustainable Development Goal Indicators in the Kyrgyz Republic. http://www.stat.kg/media/publicationarchive/4b272e5e-8986-4562-9c2f-34e70a48597f.pdf. Accessed 13 Nov 2022

National Statistical Committee of the Kyrgyz Republic (2021) Women and Men of the Kyrgyz Republic 2016–2020, 245–255. http://www.stat.kg/media/publicationarchive/b057b115-c40b-4180-ae16-28ec7e459117.pdf. Accessed 20 Oct 2022

National Strategy of the Kyrgyz Republic on Achieving Gender Equality by 2020. As amended by the Decree of the Government of the Kyrgyz Republic, dated 20 November 2015, No. 786. Centralized Database of Legal Information of the Kyrgyz Republic. https://tinyurl.com/3442nctt. Accessed 12 Nov 2022

Ribeiro V (2011) Gender relations in Kyrgyzstan and Tajikistan: a comparative study. POL 328—Politics in Central Asia Miami University, Spring

Skolisheva M (2015) Protection used in the Kyrgyz Republic: 90% of men do not want to use condoms. https://kaktus.media/doc/329937_kak_predohraniautsia_v_kr:_90_myjchin_ne_hotiat_polzovatsia_prezervativami.html. Accessed 13 Nov 2022

Sustainable Development Report (2021) Kyrgyz Republic. https://dashboards.sdgindex.org/profiles/kyrgyz-republic. Accessed 12 Nov 2022

UN Women Kyrgyzstan Country Office (2018a) Gender in Society Perception Study, Women's Economic Empowerment, October 2018. https://eca.unwomen.org/sites/default/files/Field%20Office%20ECA/Attachments/Publications/2020/04/Gender%20in%20society%20perception%20study/GSPS_Economics_ENG.pdf. Accessed 30 Oct 2022

UN Women Kyrgyzstan Country Office (2018b) Gender in Society Perception Study, Violence Against Women and Girls, October 2018. https://eca.unwomen.org/sites/default/files/Field%20Office%20ECA/Attachments/Publications/2020/04/Gender%20in%20society%20perception%20study/GSPS_VAWG_ENG.pdf. Accessed 4 Oct 2022

UN Women Kyrgyzstan Country Office (2019) Gender in Society Perception Study, Women and Labor Migration, October 2019. https://eca.unwomen.org/sites/default/files/Field%20Office%20ECA/Attachments/Publications/2020/04/Gender%20in%20society%20perception%20study/GSPS_Migration_ENG.pdf. Accessed 24 Oct 2022

UN Women, COVID-19 Impacts on Livelihoods of Women and Men in the Kyrgyz Republic, Rapid Gender Assessment, May 2020. https://kyrgyzstan.un.org/sites/default/files/2020-07/ENG_Gender%20Rapid%20Assessment%20of%20COVID-19%20impact_June%202020_final.pdf. Accessed 8 Oct 2022

UN Women, United Nations (UN) Global Database on Violence against Women, Kyrgyzstan. https://evaw-global-database.unwomen.org/en/countries/asia/kyrgyzstan. Accessed 13 Nov 2022

UN Women (2020) COVID-19 Impacts on Livelihoods of Women and Men in the Kyrgyz Republic, Rapid Gender Assessment, May 2020. https://kyrgyzstan.un.org/sites/default/files/2020-07/ENG_Gender%20Rapid%20Assessment%20of%20COVID-19%20impact_June%202020_final.pdf. Accessed 8 Oct 2022

United Nations (UN) (1966a) International Covenant on Civil and Political Rights, New York, 16 December 1966, United Nations Treaty Collection. https://treaties.un.org/Pages/ViewDetails.aspx?src=TREATY&mtdsg_no=IV-4&chapter=4&clang=_en. Accessed 12 Nov 2022

United Nations (UN) (1966b) International Covenant on Economic, Social and Cultural Rights, New York, 16 December 1966, United Nations Treaty Collection. https://treaties.un.org/Pages/ViewDetails.aspx?src=TREATY&mtdsg_no=IV-3&chapter=4&clang=_en. Accessed 12 Nov 2022

United Nations (UN) (1966c) International Convention on the Elimination of All Forms of Racial Discrimination, New York, 7 March 1966, United Nations Treaty Collection. https://treaties.un.org/Pages/ViewDetails.aspx?src=TREATY&mtdsg_no=IV-2&chapter=4&clang=_en. Accessed 12 Nov 2022

United Nations (UN) (1979) Convention on the Elimination of All Forms of Discrimination against Women (CEDAW), New York, 18 December 1979, United Nations Treaty Collection. https://treaties.un.org/Pages/ViewDetails.aspx?src=TREATY&mtdsg_no=IV-8&chapter=4&clang=_en. Accessed 12 Nov 2022

United Nations Department of Economic and Social Affairs, Sustainable Development, UN Sustainable Development Goal 5. https://sdgs.un.org/goals/goal5. Accessed 13 Nov 2022

United Nations Economic Commission for Europe and UN Women (2021) Childcare, Women's Employment and the Covid-19 Impact and Response: The case of Kyrgyz Republic. UNECE-UN Women series: Rethinking Care Economy and Empowering Women for Building back Better. https://unece.org/sites/default/files/2021-11/Childcare_WE_Covid-19_Kyrgyzstan_en.pdf. Accessed 12 Nov 2022

Urbaeva Z, Lee E, Lee Y (2019) Reproductive decisions as mediators between education and employment of women in Kyrgyzstan. Health Care for Women International. https://www.academia.edu/81609794/Reproductive_decisions_as_mediators_between_education_and_employment_of_women_in_Kyrgyzstan?sm=b. Accessed 13 Nov 2022

World Bank national accounts data 2021. https://data.worldbank.org/indicator/NY.GDP.PCAP.CD?locations=KG. Accessed 25 Oct 2022

World Economic Forum (2022) Global gender gap report 2022. Insight Report, July 2022. http://reports.weforum.org/globalgender-gap-report-2022. Accessed 23 Oct 2022

World Health Organization (2021) Sexual and reproductive health and rights infographic snapshot Kyrgyzstan. https://apps.who.int/iris/bitstream/handle/10665/349573/WHO-SRH-21.113-eng.pdf?sequence=1&isAllowed=y. Accessed 24 Oct 2022

Open Access This chapter is licensed under the terms of the Creative Commons Attribution 4.0 International License (http://creativecommons.org/licenses/by/4.0/), which permits use, sharing, adaptation, distribution and reproduction in any medium or format, as long as you give appropriate credit to the original author(s) and the source, provide a link to the Creative Commons license and indicate if changes were made.

The images or other third party material in this chapter are included in the chapter's Creative Commons license, unless indicated otherwise in a credit line to the material. If material is not included in the chapter's Creative Commons license and your intended use is not permitted by statutory regulation or exceeds the permitted use, you will need to obtain permission directly from the copyright holder.

Annex

Samarkand Declaration of the Asian Forum on Human Rights

Samarkand, 22–23 November 2018.

UN-GA-Doc, 06.02.2019, Seventy-third session.
Agenda item 74 (b) Letter dated 4 February 2019 from the Chargé d'affaires a.i. of the Permanent Mission of Uzbekistan to the United Nations addressed to the UN Secretary-General.

Outcomes of the seventieth anniversary of the Universal Declaration of Human Rights: challenges and reality;

We, participants of the Asian Forum for Human Rights,

Noting that, 2018 is the year of the 70th Anniversary of the Universal Declaration of Human Rights, as well as the 25th anniversary of the Vienna Declaration and Action Program on Human Rights, and that all human rights and fundamental freedoms are universal, indivisible, interdependent and interrelated,

Affirming our obligations to promote universal respect, observance, and protection of all human rights and fundamental freedoms for all under the Charter of the United Nations, the Universal Declaration of Human Rights, and other international human rights instruments.

Reaffirming that States have the primary responsibility for the respect, promotion and protection of all human rights and fundamental freedoms of all persons and the obligation to follow them,

Recalling that the 2030 Agenda for Sustainable Development seeks not to leave anyone behind and aims at ensuring equality and non-discrimination, putting people at the center of the development process, thus seeks to realize human rights of all.

Considering that the Sustainable Development Goals (SDGs) are complex and indivisible, ensure the balance of all three—economic, social, and environmental components of sustainable development and place an important role in realizing the human rights of all people, achieving gender equality,

Having considered that the 2030 Agenda for Sustainable Development calls on governments, parliaments and other interested parties to draft and adopt laws and programs that meet human needs, set aside isolationist strategies, protect human rights, and leave no one behind,

Welcoming the efforts of the Governments of the Asian region to implement the 2030 Agenda for Sustainable Development and national SDGs,

Recognizing the important role of the countries of the Asian region in ensuring peace, stability, and sustainable development in the region, as well as in promoting regional and international cooperation,

Taking into account the unique cultural and civilizational potential of the Asian region, which had a decisive influence on the development of many countries and entire regions,

Considering the current challenges and threats the countries of the Asian region have been being faced, and the fact that, unlike other regions, there is no regional system for the protection of human rights in Asia,

Taking into account, that national mechanisms for reporting and follow-up (NMRFs) and national human rights institutions (NHRIs) are two constituent elements of the national human rights protection system, that complement each other,

Following the discussions, hereby agreed on the following proposals and statements:

1. Within the framework of national programs aimed at the achievement of the 17 SDGs states shall seek to ensure the full compliance with all their international obligations on human rights, focusing on the principles of equality and non-discrimination based on gender, race, religious, cultural, ethnic origin, migration status or on any other ground. It is of paramount importance to take into account the gender aspects in achievement of SDGs and fulfillment of human rights.
2. States shall establish effective national mechanisms for monitoring and tracking progress on the implementation of the SDGs, as they establish similar processes to follow up on the recommendations of human rights mechanisms and ensure the implementation of quantitative and qualitative indicators on human rights in collecting, analyzing information and drafting reports on the implementation of the SDGs. States commit to building partnerships to share good practice and enhance national and regional capacities to collect, track and report on SDG implementation and human rights using quality data and statistics.
3. States shall involve all stakeholders in the design and monitoring process with the aim of ensuring a transparent, inclusive, and accountable national process for the implementation of the SDGs and other related commitments, including all three branches of the government—legislative, judicial and executive, also statistical authorities, as well as NMRFs, NHRIs and civil society.
4. It is encouraged to ensure closer cooperation with the parliaments at the national level and inter-parliamentary organizations in order to increase the capacity of parliaments, in particular with regard to allocating budget funds for the implementation of the 2030 Agenda for Sustainable Development, and strengthening the rule of law and promoting the harmonization of national legislation with international human rights obligations.

Annex 131

5. National parliaments have important functions to promote development processes, implement national plans and strategies, and ensure greater transparency and accountability at both national and global levels, also through the participation of parliamentarians in the high-level political forum on sustainable development, capacity-building and holding regular parliamentary events dedicated to the work of parliaments in the institutionalization of sustainable development goals, including the participation of civil society institutions.
6. It is recommended for states to establish partnerships and ensure cooperation between government bodies, courts, national human rights institutions, civil society and other stakeholders in the promotion, protection and realization of all human rights and fundamental freedoms, including through advisory bodies, coordinators in bodies governance and national human rights reporting and follow-up mechanisms, or through measures aimed at ensuring observance and protection of human rights and freedoms.
7. States shall strengthen the role of NHRIs established and functioning in accordance with the principles relating to the status of national institutions for the promotion and protection of human rights (Paris Principles), and of the national human rights reporting and follow-up mechanisms, including the development of inter-agency cooperation in the protection of human rights and freedoms on the basis of equality, mutual respect and mutual benefit.
8. with the participation of the representatives of civil society, including the youth, NMRFs, NHRIs, and the academia.
9. States shall involve NMRFs, NHRIs, and independent experts from civil society in inter-agency coordination mechanisms responsible for developing national development strategies and monitoring the implementation of the SDGs. NHRIs can facilitate access to remedies.
10. States shall strive to ensure respect, protection, and fulfillment of the human rights of all migrants, regardless of their migration status and in line with the SDGs.
11. The executive power plays a key role in adopting and implementing SDGs by defining national priorities, assessing the adequate resources to achieve the SDGs, proposing the budget, ensuring data collection to track progress in implementation and ensuring compliance with other national development strategies. National mechanisms for monitoring and tracking progress on SDGs should aim at improving data collection, including statistical and gender-disaggregated data, that will be used for monitoring progress in SDGs implementation as well as the implementation of recommendations of the UN human rights mechanisms. States shall encourage the creation of partnerships on qualitative and quantitative data collection and analysis in order to enhance monitoring and reporting on SDGs.
12. The administration of justice system, including law enforcement agencies, prosecutors, and especially independent judiciary and legal profession (Bar), is essential for the full and non-discriminatory realization of human rights and is an integral element of the processes of democracy and sustainable development in the framework of 2030 Agenda for Sustainable Development. In this regard,

States should pay close attention to improving the accessibility, quality, and transparency of the administration of justice, as well as the related legislation in order to bring it into full compliance with international standards on human rights.
13. NHRIs play a key role in the implementation of the SDGs in strict compliance with human rights standards, by fulfilling the authority assigned to them through international standards, in particular the Paris Principles, the Belgrade Principles, and Merida Declaration, including powers to monitor and to draft reports on the overall human rights situation in countries, the consideration of complaints, and the promotion of human rights education and enlightenment through the establishment of cooperation and mutual capacity-building and exchange of experience.
14. States shall take decisive steps to bring the legislation on NHRIs in compliance with international standards. In order to achieve this purpose, states should ensure the establishment of an NHRI according to the constitution or a statutory law, empower the NHRI with functional independence from the executive branch, provide with a broad mandate to promote and protect human rights and equip them with adequate human and financial resources.
15. NHRIs and national human rights reporting and follow-up mechanisms, being a key element of the national human rights protection system, are called upon to play the role of an important "bridge" in society—linking the parliament, government, various other government agencies, academic and research centers, civil society, international, regional and national systems for the protection of human rights.
16. NHRIs and national human rights reporting and follow-up mechanisms within their mandates, should continue their role in upholding and strengthening the rule of law, good governance, and the effective administration of justice; fighting discrimination and promoting the protection of minorities and vulnerable groups; facilitating legal and institutional reforms and improving security institutions, such as the police and prison administration, and monitoring places of detention or imprisonment. NHRIs should protect the rights of human rights defenders in line with UN Declaration on Human Rights Defenders.
17. States shall involve civil society in all decision-making processes, especially when such decisions affect the respect, protection and promotion of human rights, including their systematic participation in planning, implementing, monitoring and evaluating policies, plans, and programs related to the implementation of the SDGs.
18. States shall create a favorable environment for the free functioning of civil society organizations and independent mass media for an objective and impartial coverage of processes on implementation of the SDGs. To this end, states shall align its national laws pertaining to the freedom of expression, freedom of peaceful assembly, and associations in line with international standards. Civil society institutions are called upon to establish regional and subregional platforms, including with a focus on concrete categories of human rights.

19. For and the SDGs, States shall strive to eradicate illiteracy, direct training to the full development of human personality and to the strengthening respect for human rights and fundamental freedoms. States shall seek to enhance mutual understanding, tolerance including all categories of civil servants, judicial, law enforcement, local self-government officials, and civil society representatives. States shall include human rights education, including on women's rights, SDGs, and electoral rights, into
20. Considering that the youth is identified as the target group for the fourth stage of the UN World Programme for Human Rights Education, civil society institutions, youth organizations in the field of education and training on equality, human rights and non-discrimination, sustainable consumption to fight against food waste, and to participate in the development and implementation of national plans of action for human rights education and training.
21. To determine the ways for the establishment of the possible regional mechanisms on human rights protection in Asia, it is recommended to conduct regular consultations and forums with wide participation of all concerned parties, including NMRFs, NHRIs, academia, and civil society institutions.

We, the participants of the Asian Forum on Human Rights, emphasize the important role of regional and international intergovernmental organizations, as well as donor states in promoting the implementation of the SDGs and protecting human rights at national levels. In this regard, we urge international partners to encourage cooperation and the exchange of the best practices among states in the elaboration of national development policies, programs, and projects.

MIX
Papier aus verantwortungsvollen Quellen
Paper from responsible sources
FSC® C105338

If you have any concerns about our products,
you can contact us on
ProductSafety@springernature.com

In case Publisher is established outside the EU,
the EU authorized representative is:
Springer Nature Customer Service Center GmbH
Europaplatz 3, 69115 Heidelberg, Germany

Printed by Libri Plureos GmbH
in Hamburg, Germany